The Book of Flowers

The Book of Flowers

by

Derenik Demirjian

Translated, with an Introductory Essay
by James R. Russell

 Armenian Heritage Press
National Association for Armenian
Studies and Research

PK
8548
.D395
G5713
2003

© 2003 by the National Association for Armenian Studies and Research, Inc.
395 Concord Ave., Belmont, Massachusetts 02478
All Rights Reserved

Library of Congress Cataloging-in-Publication Data

Demirchyan, Derenik, 1877-1956.
  [Girk tsaghkants. English]
  The book of flowers / by Derenik Demirjian ; translated, with an introductory essay by James R. Russell.
    p. cm.
  Translated from Armenian.
  ISBN 0-935411-17-8 (pbk.) -- ISBN 0-935411-17-8 (pbk.)
  I. Russell, James R., 1953- II. Title.

PK8548.D395G5713 2003
891'9935 -- dc21
                          2003012067

Printed in the United States of America

This Publication Was Made Possible By a Generous Grant From the Dolores Zohrab Liebmann Fund.

Contents

Preface 1

Introduction 3

Translation 22

Armenian Text .... [51]

Preface

Several years ago Harout Yeretzian, proprietor of Abril Bookstore in Los Angeles, gave me a little book – a beautifully-printed text of Derenik Demirčyan's story, *Girk' całkanc'*. He recommended it as a work that had given particular pleasure to him. I used the text in an Armenian language class: my friend and sole pupil in the course that year, Michael Grossman, encouraged me to prepare an introductory essay, translation, and commentary for the use of students of Armenian, for readers hitherto unacquainted with the wealth of a rather obscure literature, and for those specialists in mediaeval Armenian art and lyric who are interested in the reception of these subjects amongst the native heirs of the great tradition. I am deeply grateful to the Trustees of the Dolores Zohrab Liebmann Fund, whose generous grant has made it possible for this book to see the light of day. I thank also Marc Mamigonian of the Armenian Heritage Press of the National Association for Armenian Studies and Research for undertaking its publication, and dedicate it to my teacher and friend, the dean of Armenian studies in America, Professor Nina Garsoïan. The work was done in the last months of 2001, when death and darkness cast a pall over New York City, my home, whose own bard had dreams and visions in which eyes stared and flowers bloomed, full of life, in death's midst.

with your eyes
with your eyes
with your Death full of Flowers...

Lord Lord an echo in the sky the wind through ragged leaves
    the roar of memory
caw caw all years my birth a dream caw caw New York the bus
    the broken shoe the vast highschool caw caw all Visions
    of the Lord

Lord Lord Lord caw caw caw Lord Lord Lord caw caw caw Lord

-Allen Ginsberg, *Kaddish*, 1959.

J.R. Russell,
Cambridge, Massachusetts,
January 2003.

Introduction

Derenik Demirčyan (b. Demirčōłlean; transliterated hereafter as Demirjian), February 18, 1877-December 6, 1956, was born in the Armenian town of Axalk'alak' (Akhalkalaki), now located in the Republic of Georgia, and was educated at the Nersisean school in Tiflis (1895-97), where he was a pupil of the writer Perč Přošean, and the University of Geneva (1905-1910). In Tiflis, he worked for and published in the Armenian Socialist journal *Murč* ("Hammer"), and was a member of the literary circle called *Vernatun* ("Upper Room") led by the great poet Yovhannēs T'umanean. He settled in Erevan in 1925. In 1927 he became president of the Armenian writers' union. In 1931, the Erevan House of Culture held a reception to mark the 35th year of Demirjian's literary activity: the poets Č'arenc' (Charents) and Alazan were among the celebrants offering congratulatory messages. In 1934, Demirjian became a member of the newly-formed Union of Soviet Writers: he spoke at its first congress in Moscow in October of that year, and translations of his work into Russian began to appear. In 1938 he was appointed to the committee overseeing the celebration of the millennium of the Armenian national epic of Sasun. In 1945 he received the Order of the Red Banner of Labor. He was elected a fellow of the Academy of Sciences of the Armenian SSR in 1953. He died peacefully in his home in Erevan.

The Derenik Demirjian State literary prize for prose was established in Soviet Armenia in 1980; his complete works (*Erkeri žołovacu*) were published in fourteen volumes at Erevan, 1976-1987. He began his literary life before the Revolution but flourished as a Soviet writer, starting with verse and going on to write comedies, dramas, short stories, novels, and essays. Soviet critics of the Stalin era sometimes found his approach to his subjects insufficiently political, and this led to some unfavorable criticism. Scores of Soviet Armenian writers were murdered and many more were sent to labor camps in Siberia in those times; so Demirjian fared very well. He is best known for his comedy *K'aǰ Nazar*, "Nazar the Brave" (1922), whose subject is the timid soul who accidentally kills a number of flies and is mistakenly acclaimed the slayer of thousands; and for his massive historical novel *Vardanank'*, which deals with the Christian Armenian uprising led by St. Vardan Mamikonean against the campaign of the Sasanian Persians in the fifth century to force the Armenians to return to Zoroastrianism. The journal *Sovetakan grakanut'yun* ("Soviet Literature") began serialized publication of the novel in 1943 – at a time when the Soviet government supported such expressions of ethnic nationalism in the all-out fight against the Nazi invader.[1] Demirjian treats the war from the standpoint of politics rather than religion, as a struggle for the preservation of Armenian national identity.

But in his survey of Demirjian's work, Professor Kevork Bardakjian in his magisterial bibliographical guide to modern Armenian literature devotes proportionally more space to the short story translated here, *Girk' całkanc'*, written in 1935, than to any other work. He correctly notes Kostandin Erznkac'i as a source of inspiration – much more on this below – and suggests the story was intended to tell its readers "about some of the creative principles and continuities in Armenian culture." The title suggests that the work itself is "a very special kind of *florilegium*, a repository of some of the facets of Armenian culture." Bardakjian concludes, "The work was a synthesis of Demirjian's views of the intellectual and artistic creativity of his people, a hymn to those often anonymous monks, creators of the tradition, and to the touching ways in which such treasures were fostered and handed down to posterity."[2]

---

[1] In American-Armenian propaganda art of the period, a ghostly St. Vardan Mamikonean is shown above Red Army soldiers defending the factory-scapes of a flourishing, Communist Erevan. On the politics and art of the period see J.R. Russell, *An Armenian Epic: The Heroes of Kasht*, Ann Arbor, MI: Caravan Books, 2000, Introduction.

[2] All the above biographical and bibliographical information is drawn from *Derenik Demirčyan: taregrut'yun, matenagitut'yun*, Erevan: Sovetakan groł, 1977; and from the indispensable work of Kevork B. Bardakjian, *A Reference*

As will be seen from the footnotes to my translation of the text, the story is also a kind of meditation on Demirjian's wide and careful reading of medieval Armenian poetry.

In Demirjian's story, an Armenian boy of the Van area named Zvart (Arm. *zuart'*, "joyful") sees wonderful beings in things and nature, and the villagers, thinking him possessed, pressure his parents to consign him to the care of a monastery. But the abbot, who was once a famous architect, perceives in the boy a kindred creative spirit and cares for him – soon enough, Zvart has a vision of a sunlike youth, a kind of higher self, who opens up to him the poetic talent that enables him to express his vision, and he recites a pantheistic poem about love pervading and inhabiting all the universe and its movements. For all its particular flavor and undoubted focus on the Armenian experience, "The Book of Flowers" would probably not be as powerful a literary work, if it did not address at the same time issues of general human concern – the mystery of creativity, the predicament of the artist, and the survival of art over the ages – to name a few. In the patient abbot, I am reminded of the one at Gethsemani monastery in Kentucky who ordered Thomas Merton, who had fled secular literary life, to write, knowing that the word was the newly-ordained monk's true calling, his prayer through labor, his way to the Word. Zvart's effort after his initiatory experience to express his visions as art would have been understandable, at the other geographical extremity of Christendom, to Lily Briscoe, the English painter who waited years to achieve her vision, in Virginia Woolf's novel *To The Lighthouse*. Still, Demirjian's story is particularly suffused with the colors and light of the Armenian landscape, with the rich and ornate, as well as whimsical and exotic, miniature paintings and marginal illuminations of Armenian manuscripts. The latter have often survived when men and cities have fallen to the sword and been consumed by fire, and "The Book of Flowers," in which the book itself emerges as the main character, is finally as much a meditation on time and the enigmatic survival of Armenian culture as it is an exploration of the inner, psychological features of the creative proc-

---

Guide to Modern Armenian Literature, 1500-1920, Detroit, MI: Wayne State Univ. Press, 2000, pp. 216-219, 331-334.

ess. The abrupt and tragic turn of events early in the story might remind the reader of *To The Lighthouse* of the chapter "Time Passes"; and it might not be too farfetched to compare Woolf's perennial concern with the way society prevented women from achieving their potential to Demirjian's evocation of social and monastic superstition and repression of the artist. The two writers shared, after all, a historical epoch of struggle against old prohibitions and superstitions.

Of course the differences are still fundamental and profound. Virginia Woolf wrote most powerfully in *A Room of One's Own* of the need of women for economic and social independence, without which they might never realize themselves fully. Despite the limitations she decried, Woolf was still a wealthy, privileged citizen of a free country, and she never experienced war or mass murder directly. Demirjian's environment, in these respects, could scarcely have been more different. He grew up when Armenian society had just emerged fully from the late-mediaeval social conditions of the 18th-century Near East into turbulent modernity; and he received his education during the time when the Tsarist régime was attempting forcibly to Russify the Armenians by closing schools and confiscating Church properties. This was itself nothing compared to the horrors to come of World War I and the Genocide that followed, and of the famine, disease, and chaos of the first Armenian Republic and the subsequent privations and repressions of the totalitarian Soviet system. Demirjian's writing reflects these grim facts of Armenian experience – hence, perhaps, Zvart's sudden and unrelievedly horrible fate, made still harder to bear by its brief, casual mention. But Demirjian also feels and expresses a hope that transcends the personal and private limitations of writers like Virginia Woolf: "The Book of Flowers" has a scope and depth, not of a human lifetime, but of the centuries of Armenian suffering and resurrection – the lifetime of the true hero, an illuminated manuscript, a portable garden, a book of flowers. And Demirjian's ultimate hope, also glimmering at the end of the story, is for the promise of the October Revolution so fundamentally to transform humanity that all unfreedom, injustice, and ignorance must never again darken any life. In the spring of 1917, the Russian Armenian press seems to have been unaware of the scale of the horrors in

Turkish Armenia and unwilling to give credence to reports that, as we now know, were anything but exaggerations. But articles bristle with anger against the repressive Tsarist régime and Russian great-power chauvinism: for Russian Armenians, revolution was at the top of the agenda. Though the scope of Demirjian's work embraces Western Armenian language and life, he spent his life in the urban centers of the Transcaucasus, where the varieties of Socialist revolt had been actively evolving for decades, particularly amongst the Armenian intelligentsia and working classes, so his greeting of Communism, the "red storm wind" of the end of "The Book of Flowers," seems to have been rooted in deep and genuine emotion.

Still, the terrible Stalinist purges of the 1930s must have shaken his convictions very nearly to their foundations. The remark of a soldier in "The Book of Flowers," "It is impossible to burn the book" (see text p. 43 and discussion in my note) grimly anticipates a line spoken by Woland in Mikhail Bulgakov's novel *The Master and Margarita*, "Manuscripts do not burn." The Nazi public book-burnings began immediately after Hitler's accession to power early in 1933; and by the late 1930s the Soviet authorities were to ban and secretly burn the books of their own enemies.

Some of Demirjian's stories are set in the chaos of war and genocide in Turkish Armenia and on the Russo-Turkish front of the first World War, and express the inability of people rooted in an ancient and relatively quiet way of life to comprehend the gigantic, mechanical forces of destruction that had broken upon them. "The Superfluous Man" (*Avelordə*) deals directly with the Armenians in the path of the Holocaust. In "Home," an Armenian soldier from Kilis in Cilicia deserts his Turkish army regiment at Gallipoli when he learns of the massacres and deportations. (This is the only work of fiction, to my knowledge, that brings together the two nightmarish episodes of slaughter at either end of Anatolia: the insane battle of attrition, in which hundreds of thousands of Turkish, Australian, and other soldiers died for nothing – Mustafa Kemal Atatürk commanded the Turkish defenses – and the Genocide of the Armenians that had begun and was proceeding at the same time.) The hero of "Home," Art'in, finds his home in ruins and follows the remnants of his family to Syria, where they settle. But he always feels like a foreign guest in exile, and does not find peace until his clan joins the post-World War II migration of Diaspora Armenians to Soviet Armenia. Though in the latter part of the story Demirjian mentions, in a humorous way, the mutual incomprehension caused by differences of dialect and the clash of Socialist and bourgeois customs, there is of course nothing of the real hardships and terrible repressions many of the migrants endured; and the story has a triumphant ending fully within the canonical rules of Socialist Realism.

Other stories deal with the experience of World War II – what the Soviet people called the Great Patriotic War against fascism – and "Chaconne," in particular, deals directly and powerfully with anti-Semitism and the Nazi Holocaust. Soviet Armenian soldiers died by the thousands, and many taken prisoner by the Germans tried to protect Russian Jewish comrades by claiming them as fellow Armenians. Armenian civilians living in the occupied Ukraine often sheltered Jews from the Nazis; so to many Armenians the second great war of the twentieth century was a nightmarish repetition of the holocaust of the first; and this endowed it with a particular significance that Demirjian, too, seems to have felt. He might not have known Hitler's remark "Who remembers the Armenians?" which was intended to reassure German generals that the Final Solution would not have adverse repercussions for them. Little has been written of those Armenians themselves, who could not help remembering, and who saw it happening again. The topic of anti-Semitism was at best controversial and most often taboo in Soviet literature; so Demirjian's story, which enters so compassionately into the tragedy of a people other than his own, was itself an act of moral courage.

But let us return to the refuge and relative comfort of the imaginal, sempiternal universe of manuscript art in the "Book of Flowers." Zvart's imagined scenes – of costumed people riding exotic animals and so on– are drawn, not from the large scenes of the life of Christ and the portraits of the Evangelists that comprise the formal iconographic program of Armenian manuscript art, but from the fanciful paintings, drawings and doodles that adorn the edges of the page, the marginalia. Sometimes these images are meant to illustrate a line in the text, or to provide a humorous, ironic, or ribald commentary or pun on it. This is a feature of mediaeval Christian art generally. At other times, the fanciful images are intended specifically to evoke the visionary dreams of Biblical characters– Jacob's ladder, or the four kingdoms in the Book of Daniel. So here there is a direct relationship between fantastic art and vision: it is perhaps Zvart's capacity to see things in unusual juxtapositions that predisposes him to visionary experience (hallucination with an unusual degree of subconscious meaning-content?). Christians were admonished not to try to know that which is on high, i.e., the divine mystery – cf. Jerome's mistranslation of Romans 11:20, *mē hypsēlophronei* "don't be haughty" as *noli altum sapere*. The Christian faith is itself a mystery-religion in which the central mystery is almost eliminated by being made explicit and public; so the still-necessary aspect of mystery must be relegated from the realm of the discursive and scientific to the personal, experiential, and intimate, which is comprehended by mysticism generally, but also by creative art as here. In both cases – mysticism and art – there is a reaction to tame and to institutionalize tendencies which might otherwise have the potential to change or challenge dogma. Mysticism is more or less successfully subsumed under the monastic orders. But art, as my friend Prof. William Beeman of Brown University observed once, has by its nature to push the limits. Armenian art did not evolve into secular forms of any importance; but one may observe the minor phenomenon of the attempt to co-opt fantastic images as an iconology in a very limited context – that of the Canon tables (Arm. *xoran*, lit. "canopy") with which Gospel manuscripts begin. These are frequently adorned with opulently strange images of the sort one might most often encounter in marginalia – but in this case they are often endowed with an explicit symbolic significance within the defined Christian dogma: St. Nersēs Šnorhali and others wrote explanations (*meknut'iwn*) of these.[3] When I was a boy of fifteen, visiting Erevan for the first

---

[3] The best recent study of the marginalia of mediaeval manuscripts is the late Prof. Michael Camille's *Image on the Edge: The Margins of Medieval Art*, Cambridge, MA: Harvard Univ. Press, 1992. In a paper on the Cilician Armenian poet Frik ("Frik: The Bridge of Poetry," forthcoming in R. Hovannisian, ed., *Proceedings* of the UCLA Conference on Armenian Cilicia), I suggested that the means of transmission of images of Chinese dragons and lions em-

time, I spent hours in the display room of the Matenadaran Institute of Ancient Manuscripts, captivated by the calligraphy in an unknown script and the brilliant, jewel-like pictures on the parchment pages. Demirjian had seen these same books, and imagined their makers. But, in view of his active presence in the era of genocide and revolution, I should think that their creator meant Zvart and his friends and successors to represent artistic innovators and revolutionaries who struggle, are killed or repressed, and are victorious – as progress always must be.

The poem to which Bardakjian alludes in his brief discussion of *Girk' catkanc'* is beyond any doubt the one whose Armenian text is reproduced below and followed by my English translation.[4] It is an account by the mediaeval Armenian lyric poet Kostandin of Erznka (Turkish Erzincan) of the initiatory vision he experienced in his youth: Demirjian most likely read it in a 1905 edition of Kostandin's works,[5] and it is evidently the inspiration for the boy Zvart's vision in "The Book of Flowers." In the twentieth century, the Russian writer Andrei Sinyavsky observed that "verses, rhymes, are very appropriate instruments for speaking of strange things, because of their very strangeness," allowing things to be said "that one would be embarrassed to say in a normal fashion."[6] This observation serves to highlight the difference between the

---

ployed in Armenian Canon-tables in the Mongol period, when Frik lived, would most likely have been sketchbooks of the kind known throughout Christendom then; and the evidence of East Asian material in known Armenian sketchbooks seems to vindicate this hypothesis: see Robert W. Scheller, *Exemplum: Model-Book Drawings and the Practice of Artistic Transmission in the Middle Ages (ca. 900-ca. 1450)*, Amsterdam: Amsterdam Univ. Press, 1995, esp. pp. 400-412. On the Canon-tables, see J.R. Russell in Thomas F. Mathews, *Armenian Gospel Iconography: The Tradition of the Glajor Gospel*, Washington, DC: Dumbarton Oaks, 1991.

[4]Professor Bardakjian has recently brought to my attention the publication in a Soviet anthology of an English translation of *Girk' catkanc'*. I have not seen or consulted it.

[5]H.M. Poturean, *Kostandin Erznkac'i, XIV daru žołovrdakan banastełc*, Venice, 1905.

[6]Cited in the *New York Review of Books*, Midsummer edition, 2002.

Western tradition and that of an Oriental culture. The Armenian Zvart expresses the feeling of his vision in a poem, not because the content is strange, though, but because this was the accepted medium of much artistic, religious, and other communication in a society where the minstrel, *gusan*, had played a central role. No strangeness would have attached to the poetic medium for Armenian readers of Demirjian's time, either. If anything, the alternation of prose and verse in the early sections of the story might have evoked the similar mixture of forms in the Epic of Sasun or in the Armenian version of the Alexander Romance, with its *kafa* (from Arabic *qafiya*) stanzas – far from evoking strangeness, the latter enabled a performer merely to recapitulate the plot in song, often with a sententious, didactic interpretation of the matter. These interpretations were not regarded as contradictory to the spirit of the episode thus treated: Christian morality and the romantic, even amoral matter of popular narratives were both of importance to mediaeval imagination, and were considered mutually reconcilable. But for all that, Zvart's experience, like the poem that inspired it, is unusual. It is an irreducible mystery that he sees in imagery of light (towards the end of the story, the Book itself becomes a mystic sunlight glinting on the waves of time) and can evoke only as song.

Kostandin's poem has been re-edited and much discussed subsequently, and is to be situated in a long Armenian and Near Eastern tradition of initiatory dream-visions in which the muse or angelic interpreter is a sunlike youth. The prototype probably should be traced back to the Zoroastrian past, to evocations of Sun-eyed Ahura Mazdā, of sunlike Mithra, of the fiery Verethraghna (Arm. Vahagn). The text and my translation follow.[7]

---

[7]On the background of such visions in Armenian, Iranian, and Near Eastern culture generally, see this writer's two articles, "The Dream Vision of Anania Širakac'i," *REArm* 21, 1988-1989, pp. 159-170; and "'Sleep' and 'Dreaming' in Armenian," J. Greppin, ed., *Proceedings* of the Fourth International Conference on Armenian Linguistics, Delmar, NY: Caravan, 1992, pp. 147-169. For a specific study of Erznkac'i's poem, as preserving some imagery and thematics of Gnostic poetry, see my study "The Epic of the Pearl," *REArm* vol. 28, 2003. The Cilician Armenian poet Frik had an initiatory vision, as well (see my article, "Frik: The Bridge of Poetry," *op. cit.*); and just as Moslem minstrels had to

Ոմանք շարախոսեն գինէն վասն նախանձու, թէ րրպէ՞ս խօսի սա այսպիսի բան, զի վարդապետի չէ աշակերտել. զի այլ է աշխատութն և այլ է շնորհքն ի Հոգույն, զոր ես պատմեմ ձեզ, խաղաղս տեսլեան իմոյ, զոր տեսի զարմանալի տեսիլ, մինչ ի վանք կայի Հնդեռասան ամաց, զոր տեսի այլ մի արեգակնազզեստ և լի լուսով:

Ոմանք չար են Հետ ինձ ու նաձանձով են լիմ վերայ,
Վասն իմ գրբեալ բանիս, որ առ մարդիկ երևենայ.
Ասեն թէ՝ Ոնց գրբէ բան քաղցրահամ ու մեզ կարդայ,
Որ ի մեր միջիս ընդեր կամ համեմատ իւր չրկայ:

(5) Կոյր են Հոգւով աչոք, մրտոքլիմար են, անլիմայ,
Թէ տէր ո՞վ է խելաց, կամ այս շնորհիս, որ առ իս կայ.
Ես եմ աման Հողէ 'լ ի լիս լրցւած կայ խաղիմայ,
Զոր ես խօսիմ Հոգւով, այն մեծ Տիրոջն է մանանայ:

Ով գող է այս գանձիս, ու կամ նենգով ինձ լինայ,
(10) Աստուծոյ է Հակառակ 'լ ինք դատաստան առնէ նորայ.
Ով որ ինձ միտ դրնէ ու զինչ խօսիմ ինք Հասկանայ,
Նա ես իր տամ նրշան՝ թէ այս շնորհիս որպէս Հասայ:

Ես երբ Հրնդետասան ամաց էի մանուկ տրղայ,
Ի վանք լուսումն էի, և գիշեր մի տեսիլ տեսայ.
(15) Մանուկ ի լուսեղէն յաթոռ նրստել որպէս արքայ,
Նրման արեգական է գեղեցիկ որ լոյս կու տայ:

Այնպէս ես լիր փառացն և ի լուսույն զարհուրեցայ,
Որ չրկարցի Հարցանել թէ՝ Տէր, ով ես, դանունդ ասա՛.
Երկիր պագի իրենն ի յայն պահուն ունց ինք տեսայ,

---

have an initiatory dream about Elijah/Khezr, so the Armenian Sayat'-Nova had one about St. John the Forerunner (*Surb Karapet*). On Vahagn, see my article "Carmina Vahagni," *Acta Antiqua* 32.3-4, Budapest, 1989, pp. 317-330. On Sun-eyed Ahura Mazdā, see my article "A Poem of Grigor Narekac'i," *REArm* 19, 1985, pp. 435-439. The publication of the most recent and detailed translation and study of the entire *Divan* of Kostandin Erznkac'i, the Leiden thesis of Prof. Theo Van Lint of Oxford University, is eagerly awaited.

(20) Ու իրեք խնդրրուածով Հոդոյն Հասար խոնարհեցայ:

Ասցի. Ես գունահքար, դու թագաւոր, քեզիկ մեդայ.
Ասցի. Հոգոք հիւանդ եմ, զքեզ բժիշկ ինձիկ գրտայ.
Ասցի. Ես եմ ադքատ, 'ւ յերակ բանի կարօտ կեցայ.
Շնորհէ դու այս գերոյս մասն ու բաժին ինձ և դիյայ:

(25) Նա իր սիրտն ողորմած՝ անարժանիս շոյտ քաղցրանայ,
Ելնէ ի յաթոռույն և դրնէ դոտն ի յիմ վերայ.
Կոխէ դիս և քայլէ, 'ւ այլվայր ի յիր տեղըն գրնայ.
Երբ իմ խնդիրքն եղաւ, ես մուրատով ի յուտն ելայ:

Ասցի. թող քո տեսդ ինձ արքայութիւն հերիք լինայ,
(30) Թէ գթաս յանպէտ ծառայ 'ւ յերակ քո տեսդ ինձ երևնայ,
Նա ես դայս կեանքս ունայն ուրանամ, երբ որ զքեզ տեսայ.
Երբ դիս ընդունեցար և կոչեցիր քեզիկ ծառայ:

Նա ինձ պատասխանեց, քաղցր ձայնով ասաց՝ Գրնա՛:
Նա իր բարրատն ահեղ գարհուրեցոյց դիս, որ գարթայ.
(35) Ելնեմ կապեմ դօտի ու մէն յաղօթք ես կանգնեցայ.
Խնդրի յայն սուրբ տեսույն, որ հետ մի այլ առ իս նա դայ:

Անցաւ աւուրք բազում, 'ւ ես աղօթք ի լաց կեցայ,
Չի իր պայծառ տեսույն ես հետ մի այլ փափագեցայ.
Չունի գորեէ հանգիստ ու ոչ գիշեր ի քուն մրտայ.
(40) Եդայ գերդ բզյիմար, 'ւ իսկի մարդու ի խոստ չեկայ:

Ես ոչ ի միտք բերի, թէ այս տեսիլս ինձ իրր լինայ,
Եւ ոչ զնա քննեցի, զի հասակովս ի ես տրդայ.
Երբ այլ բազում աւուրք ես ի յուսումն վարժեցայ,
Ապա զմրտաւ ածի ու դայն խորհուրդըն հասկացայ:

(45) Եղև յանկարծակի ինձ բան խօսիլ՝ ոչ ուզենայ,
Ախպես, որ ես ի յիմ խօսից շարելըն զարմացայ.
Սիրով ու մեծ յուսով ես այս բանիս ի փորձ մրտայ,
Չհոգիս փոխան տուի, 'լ ապա ես այն հոգոյն հասայ։

Իմ բանս ի յայն լուսույն եկել առ իս ինձ մանանայ,
(50) Որ իմ աշօքս ես զինք բարձր ի յաթոռ նըստած տեսայ.
Երբ որ զայս մեծ պարգևքս ի յայն լուսույն ես ընկալայ,
Նա զիմ մարմինս հոգովս իր սուրբ տեսույն գըրեմ ծառայ։

Այսօր հոգովս ուրախ եմ և ի մեծ մուրատ հասայ,
Որ ես առանց շըրթունք՝ կու խըմեմ յայն գինուն շիշայ.
(55) Սարխոշ եմ յայն սիրուն 'լ է միտքս ի հօն՝ յուր ինք լինայ.
Չունիմ շատող կարիք, ով է շարկամ որ զիս որսայ։

Ես եմ մէջ աշխարհիս զերդ ըզյիմար ի յանդիշայ.
Ոմանց թըւիմ խելօք, ոմանց խիստ խևու անիմայ.
Ոմանք շարին հետ ինձ, կըռձեն ատամն ի յիմ վերայ,
(60) 'Ի ոմանց պատեհ թըւի զարինս հեղուլ իր կամ լինայ...

Some speak evilly of me out of envy, saying "How does he recite such poetry, not having studied priestcraft?" For work is one thing and grace from the Spirit is something else, as I relate to you concerning my vision that I saw – a wonderful vision that I beheld, while I was in the monastery at age fifteen, of a man clothed in the Sun and full of light.

Some speak evil to me and are jealous of me
On account of the poetry I write that is renowned among men,
And say "How does he write such sweet-tasting poetry that he reads to us
So that among us he has no fellow or like?"

(5) Blind are they in their souls' eyes, foolish in mind, not understanding

Who the master is of wisdom or of this grace that is with me.
I am a vessel of earth and a treasure full is stored within me:
What I speak through my soul is manna of the great Lord.

Whoever is this treasure's thief or is deceitful towards me
(10) Is against God, who will Himself judge him.
Whoever inclines his mind to me and understands what I say —
To him I give a sign of how I attained this grace.

When I was a boy-child of fifteen years
I was in the monastery at study and beheld a vision one night:
(15) A luminous youth is seated on a throne like a king;
He is beautiful as the Sun that gives its light.

So by his glory and light was I terrified
That I could not ask "Lord, who are you? Say your name."
I bowed down before him in the moment I saw him
(20) And with three pleas flattened myself upon the ground.

I said "I am a sinner, you are a king, I have sinned against you."
I said "I am sick in soul, I have found in you my physician."
I said "I am poor and have ever been wanting for the Word.
Grant me, your captive, part and portion and the robe."

(25) His merciful heart swiftly sweetens towards me, the undeserving:
He rises from the throne and places his foot upon me,
Stands on me and strides, and then returns to his place.
When my request was made, I stood up and my heart's desire

I said: "Let your sight be kingdom enough for me —
(30) If you pity your worthless servant and your sight appear to me always,
Then I renounce this vain life, now that I have seen you,
When you received me and called me to be your servant."

He replied, and in a sweet voice said to me "Go!"
His mighty speech terrified me so that I awoke.
(35) I rise, I bind the girdle– and as I stood in prayer

I begged that holy sight to come to me once more.

Many days passed and I prayed in tears,
For I desired the shining sight of him another time.
Daytime has no rest, nor do I sleep at night.
(40) I was like a fool, but I confessed it to no man.

I did not ponder what this vision might be,
Nor did I investigate it, being but a boy in age.
When after many more days I was trained in learning
Then I turned it over in my mind and understood the mystery.

(45) Suddenly I could speak poetry to any man who asked for it
So that I was amazed at my own stringing together of words.
With love and great hope I began to try this art
And traded my soul for it, attaining that spirit then.

My poetry came to me – manna from that light,
(50) Him whom I saw on his high throne seated with my own eyes.
Now that I have received this great gift from that light
I consign my body and soul to his holy vision as servants.

My soul rejoices today, and I have attained my heart's desire,
For without lips I drink from that bottle of wine.
(55) I am high with his love and my thoughts are there where he dwells
And I have no need of the many who are evil-willed, who hunt me.

I am in this world in reason like a fool.
To some I seem intelligent; to others, crazy, utterly without sense.
Some act evilly against me, grind their teeth over me,
(60) And some would think it right to spill my blood wherever they could...[8]

    As to the name of the hero of our story, the word *Zuart'*, meaning "joyful, gay," is relatively modern as a proper name, and

---

[8]The ellipsis, alas, is not mine, but that of the text itself, whose end has - alarmingly, perhaps, considering the last known stanza - been lost.

may correspond in usage to the Persian male name *Khurram*, "happy."⁹ In modern Armenian it is more often than not a woman's, not a man's, name: my late teacher Ms. Zuart'arp'i (the latter part meaning the sun or sunlit sky) Tarpinian (Darbinean), for example. But the class of angelic beings called alert, Greek *egrēgoroi*, are the Armenian *Zuart'unk'*; the great circular seventh-century church whose ruins lie near Erevan's airport bore their name in the gen. pl., *Zuart'noc'* (Zvartnots). Little Zvart in our story is angelic in his gentle joy and his constant perception of otherworldly beauty in the world. And he is radiant, as is his spirit double, too; so perhaps Demirjian had in mind, when he named him, also the ancient Greek Christian hymn known in the Armenian liturgy of Vespers as *Loys zuart'*, "Joyful light."

Ալէլուիա. Ալէլուիա։
Լոյս զուարթ սուրբ փառաց անմահի, Հօր երկնաւորի սրբոյ կենարարի
յիսուս քրիստոս։
Եկեալքս ի մտանել արեգականն, տեսաք զլոյս երեկոյիս։ Օրհնեմք
զՀայր եւ զորդի եւ զսուրբ Հոգիդ աստուծոյ։ եւ ամենեքեան ասեմք
ամէն։ Արժանաւորեա զմեզ յամենայն ժամ, օրհնել ձայնիւ երգով զանուն
փառաց ամենասուրբ երրորդութեանդ։ Որ տայս զկենդանութիւն, վասն որոյ
եւ աշխարհս զքեզ փառաւորէ։

"Hallelujah, hallelujah! Joyful light of the holy immortal glory of the heavenly father, holy maker of life, Jesus Christ! We have come at the setting of the sun and seen the light of this evening. We bless Father and Son and Holy Spirit of God. And all say Amen. Make us worthy in every hour to bless in a voice of song the name of the glory of your holy Trinity, which gives life, on account of which this world, too, glorifies you."¹⁰

---

⁹H. Ačaṙyan, *Hayoc' anjanunneri baṙaran*, repr. Beirut, 1972, vol. 2, p. 216.
¹⁰*Žamagirk' Hayastaneayc' S. Ekełec'woy*, Jerusalem: St. James', 1955, pp. 540-541. I had thought it an Armenian composition; Fr. Dr. Krikor Maksoudian, Director of the Zohrab Center, Armenian Diocese, New York, kindly informed me it is a translation from Greek.

Armenian thought, steeped in the Zoroastrian reverence for light, took to this splendid hymn; and in other contexts, too, the word *zuart'* is associated with light – making the name especially appropriate for a literary character who has a dazzling, luminous vision. In the Armenian version of the Wisdom of Aḥiqar, for instance, the Assyrian prime minister counsels his decadent nephew, *Ordeak, or zuart' ē mtōk', aregakn ē lusawor ew or neng ē ew neł ē srtiw, xawar ē mt'ac'eal* "Little son, whoever is alert in mind is a luminous sun, but he who is deceitful and strait of heart is dusky darkness."[11] In 1857 the press of the Nersisean school at Tiflis (which Demirjian was to attend) published a book of adventure tales, wisdom texts, and miraculous hagiographies, *Patmut'iwn płnjē k'ałak'in yorum en bank' xratakank' ew ōgtakark' Xikaray imastnoy ew ayl bank' pitanik'*, "The History of the Bronze City, in which are the useful words of counsel of Aḥiqar the wise and other needful words." This is very likely the edition of the Wisdom of Aḥiqar that Demirjian read; and it contains also the account of the vision by a priest of the town of Artamet, near Van, of a luminous youth, in the eighth chapter, *Patmut'iwn tēr Yuskan, ew ordwoy norin Step'annosi* "The history of lord Yusik and the son of the same, Step'annos." In the text, a Moslem butcher named Yüsüf tests the holiness of the miracle-working priest Stephen by asking him to bless his "father" Kočik – in fact he is referring to the butcher's block, a tree stump (*koč*) in his shop. Stephen prays, innocently – and the Moslem returns home to find his mallet has become a live, flowering tree. Repenting and rejoicing, he comes back to be baptized as a Christian. On page 186:

Եւ ապա սուրբ վարդապետն Ստեփաննոս եմուտ ի տաճար սրբոյն Սահակայ, և արտասուալից պաշտամանք խնդրեաց յաստուծոյ, զի այնու կանխացեալ կոճին՝ բացում ցայցց առողջութիւն եղիցի։ Եւ զկնի աղօթիցն ելեալ ի տեսրան սուրբ վարդապետն, զի ճեղունք տաճարին բացան, և յերկնից սատիկ լոյս փայլատակեալ եմուտ ի տաճարն. և ընդ լուսոյն բազմութիւն զօրաց հրեշտակաց՝ և ի միջի նոցին աչեղնակերպ և զուարթատեսիլ երիտասարդ մի՝ նստեալ ի վերայ չորեքերպեան աթոռոյ, զոր երեքսրբեան քաղցրաձայն բարբառով բերեալ՝ եդին ի վերայ սրբոյ

---

[11]A.A. Martirosyan, ed., *Patmut'iwn ew xratk' Xikaray imastnoy*, Erevan: Arm. Acad. Sci., 1969, p. 101 para. 110a.

սեղանոյն։ Եւ նա ինքն Քրիստոս ձայնեալ առ սուրբ վարդապետն Ստեփաննոս՝ և քաղցր բարբառով ասաց, կատարեցան խնդրուածք քո՝ զոր Հայցեցերդ և զոր Հայցես, ով սիրելի իմ. և ապա ամփոփեցաւ տեսիլն։

"After that the priest Stephen entered the temple of St. Isaac, and with tearful entreaties asked of God that through that newly – verdant stump there be the healing of many pains. And after prayer the holy priest beheld in a vision that the ceiling of the temple opened, and light in mighty lightning-flashes from heaven entered the temple. And with the light were the many hosts of the angels, and in their midst a youth, awesome in form and of joyous appearance (*zuart'atesil*), seated upon a tetramorphic throne, which they bore with sweet singing of the Trisagion and placed upon the holy altar.[12] And he, Christ Himself, called the holy priest Stephen, and said to him in a sweet voice, 'The requests you asked for and ask, are fulfilled, O my dear one.' And then the vision withdrew." Demirjian perhaps borrowed the name Zvart and the locus of his narrative from here.

Zvart is called a butterfly, which was often an image of the soul; he is often described as *ašxoyž* "energetic, vivid, ardent;" his heart and mind are always kindled, inflamed, radiant. And it is therefore important that the youth in his vision, unlike in Erznkac'i's poem, is not of another, but of himself. It is not the higher or alien spirit-self of a Gnostic's vision, it is just his real, creative essence, fully human, the unblemished image of his luminous Creator. This self – I think Demirjian means to suggest – is unrealizable in the metaphorical and literal prison of mediaeval

---

[12]Tetramorphic, Arm. *č'orek'kerpean*, that is, a throne whose four legs are supported by the four holy creatures of Ezekiel's vision – ox, lion, eagle, man. These became the emblems of the four Evangelists and because of their quaternity were understood also to prefigure the holy Cross. See J.R. Russell, "The Four Elements and the Cross in Armenian Spirituality, with an Excursus on the Descent in Merkavah Mysticism," *Jewish Studies Quarterly*, Tübingen, vol. 4 (1997), no. 4, pp. 357-379. The Trisagion, Greek for "thrice-holy", is the Hebrew liturgy of Ezekiel's angels, which became part of the Jewish liturgy and was, like the rest of the vision, co-opted to Christian usages: "Holy, holy, holy is the Lord of Hosts!"

life. It must conceal its real intentions in metaphor, but some day it will speak openly.[13]

Another theme of importance in the story and the Book in the story is that of labor and the value and dignity of the working man. This theme is not at all surprising, as a socialist complement to Demirjian's naturalism; but he emphasizes particularly construction, the architectonic essence of the universe, and the craft of the mason (Arm. *ormnadir*, lit. "wall-layer"). It is worth recalling that many 19th-century Armenian intellectuals and social reformers (Raffi, most notably) were brethren of the ancient fraternity of the Freemasons, whose lodges in the Near East were a magnet for men involved actively in enlightenment and in democratic reform and revolution. The phrase "It is impossible to burn the book" in Demirjian's story may echo Bulgakov's oblique protest against Stalinism; if Demirjian had in mind Freemasonry, he had to be equally cryptic, since the order, to which many of the participants in the February Revolution in Russia had belonged, was banned by the Bolshevik régime and survived in secret till the dissolution of the Soviet Union.

Transliteration and orthography, etc.

For most technical transliterations and discussion I employ the pre-Soviet orthography of Armenian and the Hübschmann-

---

[13]The abbot asks Zvart to provide a theological exegesis of the naturalistic, pantheist poem he has just recited, which has angered the monks. The clear implication is that an actual mediaeval poem whose concluding portion explains the Christian symbolism of the preceding images of nature – and Kostandin Erznkac'i and others wrote such poems, whilst many more of unknown authorship achieved the status of folk songs – is intentionally self-censored, as it were, to protect the poet against accusations of heresy. The assumption must then be that the authors of such verses were Christians by fear rather than conviction. I think this is an anachronistic projection of Stalinist conditions backward into an age whose spiritual complexion was almost entirely forgotten. This kind of presumed concealment is different from what I have in mind, which is more personal and particular to the poet's sense of his own individuality and gift.

Meillet system of transliteration of it – the scholarly standard – of the *Revue des Études Arméniennes*, Paris. Diaspora Armenians – the numerical majority of the nation – employ this older orthography almost universally, and have taken to calling it "Mesropian," after St. Mesrop Maštoc', the inventor of the Armenian alphabet. This is a good designation, since Armenian tradition is entirely on their side. But Demirjian was a Soviet writer and the text here is in the simplified orthography still used in Armenia– simple if you know, for instance, that in it *sēr* "love" and *ser* "cream" are both spelled with the same short -e-. The ecstatic cry in Zvart's poem (p. 23 of the Armenian text) that the world, men, the sun, and the flowers are all *ser* is not an advertisement for the dairy industry. But this is the official system of orthography in the post-Soviet Republic of Armenia, so if you are reading Eastern Armenian you had better get used to it. Names are simplified in the English: Zuart' stays, phonetically, Zvart, since he has no exact Anglo-Saxon equivalent, except perhaps the good English proper name Gay; no longer really usable;[14] but for other names from Christendom and the Classical tradition, Łunkianos is Lucian (whose namesake came from ancient Armenian Samosata anyhow); T'adē, Thaddeus (Apostle to Edessa, which also has very strong Armenian associations); and so on. Footnotes, unless otherwise indicated, are mine. I have striven in the translation to stay close enough to the original Armenian to be of service to the student, but where literalism would do violence to English, I have tried to err on the side of accuracy of meaning and fluidity of style. The pagination in parentheses corresponds to that of the Armenian text, for which I've chosen the edition Derenik Demirčyan, *Girk' całkanc'*, Erevan: Sovetakan groł ("Soviet Writer") publishing house, 1985.

---

[14] The name now has obvious sexual overtones, though; and my pupil Rachel Goshgarian informs me that her aunt Susie from Beirut uses Arm. *zvart'* to mean "homosexual" – a calque, no doubt, on English "gay."

Translation

THE BOOK OF FLOWERS

(5)

Let my hand wear out and turn to earth:
This writing, a memorial, remains.

(Mediaeval)

The flowers are fires; the fruits are precious stones– so he saw it – and the birds and beasts, costumed jesters, play out the fables from the lives of kings, princes, and commoners that his grandmother had told him. For him the steep river banks wore frowns, and the mountains were the waves of Lake Van in a storm.

"See!" – he said once, "a boy has mounted a lion and is riding him."

"Where? Where?" cried his fascinated playmates, running over.

(6)   Zvart pointed out the humps of rock in the plain and ran off laughing down the street.

They stared and saw nothing in those rocks. And they chased after Zvart to beat him for having deceived them. But they reached him on a hill hunched over a flower. And as they were preparing to hit him, he laughed, cupping the flower's satiny head and showing them:

"The priest, the priest, cowl on his head, goes nodding to the abbey."

And with comic gestures he performed a whole puppet show, making the flower dip its head this way and that, making it sparkle in his hand. The boys, forgetting the beating they had been about to administer, laughed and then looked at him in astonishment:

"What kind of kid is he?"

Once they were sitting on the cliff above the river. Zvart was already telling a story:

"I went down the gorge to the riverbank. A girl inside the foam whispered to me, 'Come, Zvart, come, come!' I went. She took me far away, to the river bottom. There were palaces decorated with lovely stones and pearls."[15]

"You're lying!" yelled one of his friends, smacking him on the head with the flat of his hand, and again the boys jumped on Zvart to beat him up. But Zvart fled home. They threw rocks after him.

(7) And at home he was already recounting to his parents and the neighbors how golden camels had been passing through the valley. There was a monkey seated on one with a cock made of gems in its hands; and the lead camel had on a golden cope. A rose with a moon-face framed by the flaming petals rode on its back.

His parents and the neighbors listened, casting sad and meaningful glances at each other. One of them shook his head.

"May you find salvation in God, my child!"

The evening scattered violets over the village, the riverbanks opposite, and the orchards in the gorge. Later, when Zvart was asleep, their neighbor, the old woman Sandukht, put her face close to Zvart's mother's:

"Missus Shen, your boy's sick, possessed by devils."

And the old man neighbor Gadisho[16], a severe-faced, clean-living man, cut her off with words that brooked no contradiction:

---

[15] The goddess in the foam could be Nanē/Anahit: see Ch. 7 of my *Zoroastrianism in Armenia*, Cambridge, MA, 1987. In Armenian epic the mother of the heroes of Sasun is Covinar /Dzovinar/, whose name includes the word *cov*, "sea"; and she becomes pregnant by drinking handfuls of a milky liquid that spout from a rock in lake Van. The latter is, of course, in Zvart's homeland. Covinar's elder son, Sanasar, descends to the lake-bottom, to a gemlike chapel like Zvart's, where he acquires his magic weapons and marvellous steed. See Artin K. Shalian, tr., *David of Sassoun*, Athens, OH: Ohio University Press, 1964.

[16] This is a Syriac name, Gad 'Išō, meaning "Jesus is (my) glory".

"Dedicate him to the Holy Sign!"

Zvart's mother grieved. His father looked grim.

And on that clear evening a thousand years ago, when the house cricket was chirping in its familiar way in a crack in the wall, Zvart's parents decided to take him away and dedicate him to the monastery of the Holy Sign.

(8)   Spring breathes deep in the Armenian mountains. The day is limpid, and the spring peacefully wells up. Zvart's family and the villagers are on a pilgrimage to a mountain monastery. They trudge on in line, on carts, on foot. Zvart is sitting on a cart and observing the villagers' new clothes, and one of them seems to him to be wearing a panther's skin.[17] He laughs at him, "Where are you going, honored sir? You've become a panther, sir!"

And his laughter rings like a bell.

"Honored sir" stares coldly at Zvart's father and shakes his head. His mother wipes her eyes. Zvart wriggled towards the yoke to sit at the head of the cart, next to uncle Manuk. Uncle Manuk hugged Zvart to him and handed him the long switch. Zvart began to drive the oxen. Then suddenly he pointed at the eye of the ox and showed it to uncle Manuk.

"Look, uncle! Look!"

"What is it, little one?"

"Look, it's night in the eye of the ox!" Uncle Manuk laughs.

The cart creaked down into a green valley and started to squeak. Uncle Manuk sang:

The little star from heaven, down, loves the little fish in the sea...
Oh, the little star cannot come down; oh! the little fish cannot go up high...[18]

---

[17] Perhaps like the Georgian *Vepqis tqaosani*, "Man in the Panther's Skin" of the great epic poet Shotʻa Rustaveli.

[18] In Persian, the moon is *māh*; the fish upon which the earth rests, *māhī*: the whole sublunar world is thus "from the fish to the moon." The Armenian verse plays upon the pair, who are in Persian a rhyme. The longing of a fish for the heavenly orb need not be in vain in all metaphors, though: Gregory the Great evoked the monastic as a fish: he swims in this world, but can leap from it into the sky. The most famous fish in Armenian mediaeval art is the one hanging

(9)   Zvart listens, and his eyes shine with interest like jewels.

"Uncle, does the little star love the little fish a lot?"

"A lot!" replies uncle Manuk with a mighty sigh.

"Uncle, then will the little star never come down at all, to be with the little fish?"

"No, little one, no," sighs uncle Manuk.

"Is heaven far?"

"Very far..."

Zvart is immersed in the sea of his thoughts: Why can't the little fish go up to heaven itself? But at that moment the brook seizes his attention: stitching its waves on the wind, it makes scores of needlework ribbons. And to either side, luminous fountains stream down from the steep rocks.

A peninsula, the abyss dropping off to either side. A blackened monastery looks down from there, severe and beautiful. Its sharp dome strains heavenward like a drawn bow. The pilgrims mill around it.

Suddenly Zvart pointed to the monastery wall with his finger and nudged his father:

"Dad! Dad! Look who's standing under the tree holding a pomegranate!"

"Where?"

(10)   "On the wall," says Zvart, peering interestedly at the wall.

His father, the pilgrims – all look with pained amazement at the monastery wall. There's nothing there. The monastery is built tall and its stones are dressed smooth. The lines of cracks play across the wall. Zvart sees a man in these cracks and laughs with pleasure.

"Ha ha! Little brows over his eyes..."

But the people surrounding him are already terrified. More pilgrims gathered round and stared in fear at Zvart, who was retracing the lines in the air with a rapid finger.

"He's giving the pomegranate to a doe. Do you see her antlers?"

---

from a handsome young angler's line, in a margin of the Haghbat Gospel, with the artist's fond plea, "Sheranik, whenever you come, bring a fish!"

The pilgrims make the sign of the Cross over their faces. Zvart's mother weeps; but his father, deeply affected, shuddering, grips Zvart by the hand. Only the abbot looks contentedly at Zvart.

The neighbor of Zvart's family whispers in the abbot's ear:

"They appear to his eyes all the time, holy father, just like a dream."

"Let us take refuge in the source of grace," murmurs the abbot.

The pilgrims and his fellow villagers look sorrowfully at Zvart and pity him. Zvart must stay in the monastery; he is to be dedicated to the monastery. He will never see their home again.

(11) The service began. It is as though the sound of ringing camel bells were ascending out of the profound abyss, their echo clanging from within. The pilgrims – excluding the women – entered the sanctuary.

The blackened, dusty arches spread their wings above like dark eagles. The shadows were already thickening in the corners. A lamp wavers weakly in the depths of the apse, like a star swimming in fog. The black-garbed monastics growl some sort of prayers in guttural voices. And the corners are sad, sad as the closed eyes of a corpse.

Zvart's soul is oppressed. He looks in fright at the floor, not daring to raise his eyes.

The service ended. They took Zvart to the apse and brought him up to a terrible corpse whose face was a leathery mask, who had a dead man's dead beard and fingers of bone. His cheek and the sunken depression of one eye were burnt by wax. He glared hideously out of his frame at Zvart. They took Zvart up to the dead man.

"Kiss him, kiss him," they hissed after him.

... The billows of water splashed, sloshed, long, from far away, from the deep. A great fish is crying: "*Vossh, voossh,* Zvart, my boy, *voossh!*"

Zvart opens his eyes. What is this? Where am I?... His father sits at his head; his (12) mother, by his side, beating her knees. The pilgrims are ranged along one side; and at his feet sits an old man of marble, who looks peacefully at Zvart, and with his look resembles, yes, just that old-man cloud I saw walking, back bent, across the blue heaven, somewhere.

At dusk Zvart's family and all the pilgrims departed. They all went away, the darkling plain remained, the tenebrous monastery, the stars streaming ice in heaven. The monastery courtyard became strait, fell silent as a gravestone, and in its midst was buried the lively butterfly – little Zvart.

Far, far away, where Zvart's family and the villagers had gone, the valley was filled with a turquoise haze. That was the way home. Zvart looked sorrowfully in that direction and groaned, his heart breaking. The abbot's acolyte took him to the abbot's cell, where he curled up on a sheepskin. The abbot sat down before the light of an oil lamp, picked up a leatherbound black book and, huge eyes fixed on the book, began to murmur under his breath. He was like the sea, alien and misty. Zvart looked at him, at the book. The abbot was lingering over one page, and on it appeared an arch gleaming with gold, sky-blue columns, and flowers. Zvart felt sad when he saw the flowers. That reminded him of the flowers of their plains and valleys. Suddenly the lamplight, the old man, the book, all of it fractured in (13) teardrops – they burst from Zvart's eyes. He began to sob. Why had they brought him, left him in this strange and silent place? When were they coming to take him away? Was he never again to see his parents, his friends? They had left him and gone. He cried with his whole heart. In the night, a fever came upon him. He began to burn in its heat. Water began to seethe in his ears, an avalanche of flowers came and roiled in his eyes. He buried his parched lips in the waters, drinking insatiably, but the more he drank, the more thirst scorched him. For some days he was unconscious of everything. Only a white winter, the abbot, would fill up the cell and later disperse. The old man observed him placidly, and waited.

And one day Zvart opened his eyes. He drew breath quietly, an icy sweat on his brow. He had recovered. The acolyte brought him soup and ice-cold spring water.

Zvart got better, but he began imperceptibly to deteriorate. The scents of home, arriving on the wind and with the flowers, filled the porch of the monastery and drew him away to his distant home, to his playmates. The mountains receded, darkening blue, towards that home, the swallows soared thither, the clouds floated there – they were swans ridden by snow-white girls. Zvart would sit beneath the battlements, on the edge of the gorge, and stare (14) in the direction of their home, towards the mountains and plains. The evening would descend intimately, caressing his burning eyes, and Lucian the acolyte would find him sleeping on the cliff-edge. He would wake him up and take him back to the cell.

And in the winter the snowflakes soared over the abyss like doves, and in his mind Zvart played with them, playing and later going back, entering the cell, he curled up on the sheepskin, slept.

Lucian the acolyte was a destitute youth, but boundlessly kind. He greatly pitied Zvart and became attached to him. When his heart was chilled by the cold stares of the monks, Zvart would seek him. Lucian had a warmth, a spark of life. He was the only one who gave his heart to Zvart.

He seemed to comfort Zvart. Thereafter, when Zvart was stretched out on his sheepskin, he would gaze quietly at the old abbot, who wrote, sleeplessly, ceaselessly, on parchment. What was he writing? In what thoughts was the profound old man immersed? Zvart's thoughts wandered around the old man, strayed, returned again to him. The abbot was an unusual man. He – that self-contained, profound man – fascinated Zvart to the utmost degree. Who was he, really? Lucian had heard, and he told Zvart. The abbot had once been an (15) architect and philosopher. He had built monasteries, halls, fortress walls. Now, when his bodily strength had waned, he had entered the monastery to occupy himself with philosophy. The monks did not respect him, since he had not come to the monastery through spiritual fervor, he was not one of the "spiritual ones"; he was one of the "corporeal ones."

What did that mean? Zvart was still more inflamed with curiosity, that he might understand the man. And during the hours of instruction, when he and Lucian sat before the abbot, their legs folded under them, Zvart, his eyes wide open, listened, lost to his own thoughts, to that infinite man. Only he did not yet comprehend well his original, unheard-of thoughts. He only saw before him a creature deep as the sea, whom he heard with insatiable desire – but in a strange language. Zvart felt a kind of intoxicating ascension.

Outside the cell, in the endless hall of nature, there is a splendid reception. The heavenly torch is kindled, and the mountains and deep valleys are resplendent in the holiday light. The birds soar in heartwrenching delight through the air. The world celebrates the noblest thing: life and its happiness.

The abbot is seated in the cell, fingering his rosary philosophically. Zvart and Lucian, (16) seated cross-legged, knee to knee, are studying some passage. A buzzing bee severs the golden pillar of light and fills the cell with the joy of life.

Suddenly the sun's glow darkened before the door. Lucian looked up and saw a tall man in the doorway. He bent his hunched back below the lintel, sticking in his curly goatish beard, fixed Zvart with the keen gaze of an eagle, and bowed before the abbot. Then he presented a book to him with the practiced gesture of a talented hand. Lucian and Zvart craned their necks to look at the book. On the pages, the text alternated with precisely-drawn depictions of the monastery and other buildings, each picture illuminated around its edges. Zvart understood that he had illuminated the book for the abbot.

"The holy father wrote the text and drew the pictures of the buildings, but Thaddeus copied it and illuminated the pages." Lucian hissed the incomprehensible words into Zvart's ear.

The abbot looked calmly at the book, sighed, and then turned to the book's illuminator with the dreamy expression of a man departing from this world.

"Now I'm prepared to go to my fathers, Thaddeus: behold this my labor and testament."

(17) The illuminator, Thaddeus, kissed the abbot's right hand and went out.

The abbot regarded Zvart and Lucian with a gentle smile and began to read his work in a loud voice. He was carried away with his own thoughts, and as he began to read it was hard to tell whether it was for himself he was reading, or for the instruction of Zvart and Lucian. "The world is an edifice and the work of builders," the abbot turned the page and recited: "The edifice is city, and the edifice is speech, and the edifice is mind."

Then he indicates heaven and earth, the monastery building, its façade, its "mind." He explains the art of cosmic architecture.

Zvart bursts into flame. The magnificent pictures trace themselves in his eyes, filling in their colors. Hammers clang, severe-faced workers in stone cut the rocks, erect splendid cities whose towers soar heavenwards. Lush gardens bloom suspended over the abysses.

"Nature does work, the tree constructs, the ant is a builder. Be ye also builders and makers, as men of earth, and love labor, for building and labor are holy..."

"Tyranny passes away, thrones and kingdoms crumble to dust, but the maker remains..."

(18) The old man becomes profounder in Zvart's eyes. He is transfigured into a man replete with miracles. His sere habit melts away and beneath it emerges a "man of the earth" whose mind is busy with a great architectural passion and dream. Zvart looks out of the cell into the "world." And in that illimitable edifice, where the birds weave silken nests, the ants construct their dwellings, all the world represents a titanic building project with heaven as its tower, the torch of the sun suspended above it, with the mountains its pillars and the gorges its niches.

Zvart is in torment, tossing sleeplessly through the nights. An incomprehensible desire tortures him. He does not know its source and what sort of desire it is, whether it is within him or outside, somewhere else – he doesn't know.

Lucian notices his torment and wants to help him.

"Read, Zvart, read," he suggests, encouraging him.

Zvart looks at Lucian with a dreamy sadness.

"I'm ignorant, Lucian. My mind is weak. When will I understand what I am?"

(19) "Be patient, Zvart, the lord of grace will come, you will receive grace, and your mind will be kindled."

"What does receiving grace mean?"

"Receiving grace is when he tells you what you want and what you must do."

"Who is the lord of grace?"

Lucian relates incomprehensible things – things he's heard but hasn't understood himself. That lord of grace is a light, that's what Lucian's heard from the abbot.

"Light?" Zvart is scared. "Will it come in the night, in the dark, when I'm all alone?" He thinks continually with unease about this being.

Zvart walks along the edge of the gorge full of these thoughts, the sun of spring dissolving over the rocks, flowers, waters; and Zvart sees things in them beneath their outward form that change them, turn them into breathing, rational beings with whom he speaks within himself in a secret language hidden even from him. He sees them everywhere, in the clouds, on the walls, in the dark. They move, take human shapes, converse with him, laugh, and call him.

Zvart traced their shapes, willy-nilly, in the air. But just as soon as he enfleshed them (20) in mental outline, in the air, they fled swiftly into unbeing and there remained only other things where they had been: words, words of flame that whispered in his ear.

They whispered, whispered, and were lost. Then they came back, again and again...

Zvart is tormented, he desires something, somewhere...

An arched, high-domed room. Zvart stands alone, below, listening to the silence. Tar-eyed night stares down from heaven, tenderly, through the windows.

It is dark in the dormitory, and sad. Only outside, in the gorge, the sleepless river rushes plashing, and in the valley a bat twitters.

Suddenly the seemingly limitless wall of the room cracks, from very far away, and there enters – who? – himself, Zvart. Zvart is not surprised. Has he not seen himself many times, in wellsprings, in dew? He had eyes of sunfire that flashed like precious jewels. The regard of those eyes transfixed Zvart with fear. (So he had had within him a thing of such terror.)

And he dared not look up at him. But a power stirred Zvart to look upon him. And now, when he raised his eyes, he fell to the floor, prostrate with terror. He remained long thus, fallen, and Zvart does not remember what happened after that.

(21) He felt only that the being came up to him and, bending down, placed its hand upon his shoulder. He felt it incline, for it was whispering, but what it whispered was inexplicable, song-like, sweet.

Zvart listened, and was lulled. The whispering stretched out like the tune of a song. In his imagination Zvart played the melody and it assumed the words and tempo that Zvart wished.

Zvart awoke. It was still night. Sweet sleep was dragging him back. Only once did Zvart open his eyes, and through the door of the cell left ajar he looked at the sky. A bright star, like molten gold, quivered in the raw predawn lightening blue. But the wonderful whisper was still flowing into his ear.

Then he awoke again. A swallow was singing psalms in the eaves of the monastery. It was the very same whisper whose sweet speech he had heard.

Zvart went outside, walked to the edge of the gorge, and began to move from rock to rock. The rays of the sun were just painting afresh the rocks' grim pillars. The river wound its strange way through the floor of the gorge. In its song could be heard the whisper of the dream.

Suddenly Zvart reflected on who it had been... Had it not been himself? But just as in the dream he thought it was himself. Who was he?...

(22)   And he noticed that he was himself continuing that whisper, that he himself was the whisperer.

And he understood that the being in the dream was himself. (But surely two beings are not the same one...)

And suddenly Zvart woke up into wakefulness. He felt speech. His heart was perishing with an incomprehensible longing. He longed to speak, to speak out loud, to give voice to song, in solemn celebration – perhaps even in front of a crowd.

And he began to murmur a recitation in a low voice. Multifarious images.

The monks were all gathered in the spring sun at the foot of the walls, looking into the gorge. Suddenly they saw Zvart tottering over the abyss.

"He's drunk, he'll fall over into the chasm!" shouted one of the monks, and ran over and seized Zvart.

Zvart stared at them with eyes aflame and began to pant, his lips trembling. They brought him to the door of the abbot's cell. The abbot emerged.

"What's wrong with you? Are you sick, my little son?"

He held his forehead: it was hot. Zvart was breathing heavily, as in a fever, and stared dreamily at the abbot, who stroked his brow and gently commanded, "Speak, my boy. Tell us something. What are you thinking?"

"Speak, speak!" urged the monks.

(23)   Zvart began to speak to them, to the abbot, and suddenly flashed like a lightning bolt and started to declaim. He felt more clearly that he must say all that filled him; he took heart and enthusiastically released his fire. He began an epic ode, about how he saw a dream, how grace came and filled him, how now he could recite whatever any man might desire.

He recited like one possessed, the words tumbled out unimpeded, he saw nothing: spring is coming, it calls out to the earth, the earth awakens, it calls the other flowers, crying "Awake, awake! How long will you sleep in the earth? Awake! Fill the world with joy."[19]

Mountain and valley fill with flowers, and
Clapping, its clapping resounding, laughing,
The world winds a diadem round its head,
The marigold[20] puts on purple,
The *dzarurik* daubs its eyes with antimony.[21]

---

[19] Here Demirjian cites Kostandin's verse, which itself is an allegory of Christ's coming as the spring of the world's resurrection. The virgins of Matthew 25 are to be wakeful and prepared with their lamps for the coming of the bridegroom, even at midnight. Cf. also Ps. 57.3, "Awake, awake, my heart!" used by St. Nersēs Šnorhali in his hymn for the dawn, Zart'ik', zart'ik' p'ar̄kim. It was intended to replace the pagan song to the rising sun he heard his bodyguards singing on the ramparts of the fortress of Hr̄omklay; and later it became popular also with pilgrims to the home of the saint.

[20] Arm. *ghatifa*, from Arabo-Turkish *qatifa*. Demirjian's note: The silk of which the women of Erzerum used to weave their holiday clothes was also called by this name. Demirjian took the flower – and the line, too – from the poem by David of Saladzor cited below.

[21] Fr. Łewond Al išan, *Haybusak kam haykakan busabanut'iwn*, Venice: S. Lazzaro, 1895, p. 269, no. 1179, is unable to identify the flower *dzarurik*, which he finds mentioned in a poem by Dawit' Salajorec'i: *Ciln u clvayn u carurik, surmay en k'ašer ač'erun*, "Every tendril and flower and *dzarurik* have painted antimony round their eyes." David, a native of village of Saladzor near Erzerum, was born *ca.* 1630, and died around the turn of the eighteenth century. He married, and named his daughter Nr̄anay (probably from *nur̄n*, "pomegranate"): in 1663 she died. He became a celibate priest and wrote a lament for her which begins with the line *P'ar̄k' k'ez t'agawor p'ar̄ac'*, "Glory

And love is the world, men are love,
Love is the Sun; love, the flower,
(24) The birds of all the heavens are love,
And by love all become beautiful.

The monks listened like stones, sunk in darkness, echoless, cold. Only the wickedest of their number, dull-faced Azaria, asked – protested, in a voice embittered by envy – "How does he say these words? For he is no priest."[22]

---

to thee, O king of glory." His poem *Govasank' całkanc'*, "The praise of flowers," contains also the line *Łatifan al ē nerkuel nman behez u ciranun* "The marigold has been painted in crimson, like satin and purple." Demirjian would have read the edition of the poem in the journal *Banasēr*, 1901, pp. 89-97 (cited by Abp. Norayr Połarean, *Hay grołner*, Jerusalem: St. James', 1970, pp. 563-565); and it will have served, therefore, as the primary inspiration for Zvart's song. A full, critical edition of Salnajorec'i's poem, in which the line on the marigold is line 53; and the one on the *dzarurik*, line 63 - is now available in Hasmik Sahakyan, ed., *Uš mijnadari hay banastełcut'yunə*, vol. 2, Erevan: Arm. Acad. Sci., 1987, pp. 350-358. The image of the flowers clapping comes also from an alliterative pattern in David's poem, line 57: *Cap'cap'n cap' tay, cicałi... /Dzap'dzap'en dzap' da, dzidzaghi/:* "The *dzapdzap* flower claps and laughs". But this and the image of a woven diadem have older roots still, in a poem on the Nativity by St. Grigor Narekac'i, tenth century (See J.R. Russell, "A Mystic's Christmas in Armenia," *Armenian Review*, Summer 1987, vol. 40, no. 2-158, pp. 1-13). David probably used the flower *carurik* because its name contains Arm *caroyr*, "antimony", and has the sound *dz-* he needs for his alliterative play. For antimony itself he employs Persian *sorma*. The theme of the various flowers waking and gathering to welcome the newly-born Christ of the metaphorical spring (or the reborn Christ of the literal season) is not new in Armenian poetry. Yovhannēs T'lkuranc'i employs it; and David, who adopted Yovhannēs' chosen self-deprecatory epithet *xew*, meaning something like "love-crazed," has probably received the theme from the works of the earlier poet (on whom see J.R. Russell, *Yovhannēs T'lkuranc'i and the Mediaeval Armenian Lyric Tradition*, Univ. of Pennsylvania Armenian Texts and Studies 7, Atlanta, GA: Scholars Press, 1987).

[22] These are precisely the words of his detractors that Kostandin Erznkac'i repeats in the poetic account of his vision.

The abbot upbraided him: "Don't blame him – his thoughts well up by themselves, and they are brilliant. And this boy is wiser than a priest..."

The chastened monks stared, all of them dumbstruck, at Zvart.

And Zvart noticed how Azaria, agitated by envy, who wished to hatch some plot against him, had turned yellow with envy. The others scowled – some ashamed, some hastening to hide from the abbot's eyes, and maybe Zvart's too.

The abbot released Zvart and ordered the monks to disperse to their cells. They departed, full of enmity towards Zvart. They hated Zvart. And at every opportunity they attacked him, scolded him, got angry at him. Zvart didn't understand them: he would look at them, smiling, and pass by.

(25) "He's making a laughingstock of us!" the monks would fume, foaming at the mouth with fury – against the abbot, who had taken a madman under his wing.

They began to plot a campaign of persecution against him. They accused him: "He's a heretic, and instrument of evil, he is writing a demonic book. It must be burned!"

The abbot found out about all this and was deeply sorrowful. He felt his own death. To whom would his half-finished ideas and works, the spirit of his buildings, remain? Lucian was still untutored; Zvart, too young. To whom was he to leave his bequest? There was darkness and the wasteland on all four sides.

One day the monks, with Azaria at their head, laid siege to the door of the abbot's cell. They had come to demand that he expel Zvart, since the boy was polluting the sanctuary with demonic thoughts.

The abbot emerged from his cell.

"By what right, O unrighteous ones?" he asked, in a sad, protesting voice. "See his grace, his thoughts!"

"Let him come out and talk again, and we'll show you his sin!"

The abbot told Zvart to come out.

"Come, little son, come and justify yourself."

Zvart came out and looked at the monks with a smile. Now, say a word before men,

(26) let them judge you. Zvart thought for a moment, and then he was transformed. He began to recite. About what? Here is what he said:

Spring came, the flowers teemed,
The violet gathered all the flowers
And made a plot against the rose:
They determined to kill the rose, lest
The rose come, in crimson adorned,
And capture the attention of all
And all gaze upon the red rose,
And they remain obscure.
The *horot-morot* [23] called to the spring snowflake;
The spring snowflake, to the lily;
The lily, to the waterlily,
The watermint,[24] to the narcissus,
And to every flower on the face of the earth,
That they come and cut down the red rose.
Suddenly the nightingale's voice rang out,
And in his green tent the rose awoke,

---

[23] The flower bears the Middle Iranian forms of the names of Haurvatāt and Amərətāt, the Zoroastrian Holy Immortal beings Health and Immortality, who preside over the sacred creations of the plants and waters. Armenian maidens on the eve of Ascension Day would sprinkle its blossoms into a pot of water and perform a divinatory game of lots on the morn: see J.R. Russell, *Zoroastrianism in Armenia*, Harvard Iranian Series 5, Cambridge, MA, 1987, ch. 12; and J.R. Russell, "Zoroastrian Elements in the Book of Esther," in S. Shaked and A. Netzer, eds., *Irano-Judaica II*, Jerusalem: Makhon Ben-Zvi, 1990, pp. 33-40, for the possible relationship of the Zoroastrian antecedent of the Arm. Christian rite to the holiday of Purim in Judaism.

[24] Arm. loan from Pers., *susambar*: The name of the flower is immortalized in the sweetest and most fragrant song of Sayat' Nova, *Ašxaruməs ax č'im k'aši, k'ani vur ǰan is inj ama*, "I will not sigh in this world, as long as you are my love": *Hutov hil, mixak, darič'in, vart', manišak, susanbar is ,/ Karməragundašti całik, hovtac'šušan is inj ama* "In scent cardamon and clove, cinnamon and rose, violet, watermint thou art, / Red in hue, bloom in the plain, lily of the valley thou art for me" (M.H. Hasrat'yan, *Sayat'-Nova*, Erevan: Haypethrat, 1959, p. 37, no. 24).

Unwound his green shroud,
And put on his fiery purple.
The flowers fled and scattered, some for shame,
(27) Some perplexed, some concealed themselves and mourned,
And some became yellow with fear.

    The rose adorned his garden, the nightingale came and sat beside him, became drunk on his sweet smell, and sang aloud:
Love is the tree; love, the rose-
Love is the bird's song on the tree-
Love is the rose; love, the nightingale
Who sits in love over the rose.
Were there no love in my heart,
I would not hang from the rose's thorn;
If love is parted from me,
May the cold and the wind take me away.

    The rose desires the nightingale and asks the nightingale to kiss him, and displays his heart, which is yellow within. That is his anguish. He complains:
They will reap him, carry him off
And brew a tonic for the sick:
That is why his heart is yellow.[25]

---

[25] Arm. *dełˊ* is "medicine"; *dełin*, "yellow" (both related to Gk. *thallos*, "green", it is essentially a plant-color, and the first tonics were herbal). Gk. *pharmakon* meant both medicine and poison, as did Arm. *dełˊ* in ancient usage. Sayat' Nova sang to his beloved, *Inčʻ konim hekʻimən, inčʻ konim ǰaren: kʻu təvacən uriš dił ē, uriš dił* "What will I do with a doctor or a cure? What you have given me is another medicine, another medicine," for *ērum ē məhlamən, čʻē lavnum yarēn* "the salve burns and the wound doesn't heal": love bestowed is a poison against whose wonderful agony God and nature contrive no bezoar. (See Hasratʻyan's ed. of Sayatʻ Nova cited, p. 39, no. 26.) Pushkin's facetious early quatrain on the subject shows how trite the idea had become, long ago: *Nadpis' na stene bol'nitsy Vot zdes' lezhit bol'noy student; / Ego sud'ba neumolima. / Nesite proch' medikament; / Bolezn' lyubvi neizlechima!* "Inscription on the Wall of a Hospital. Here lieth a sick student. / His fate is irrevocable./ Take the medicine away: / The sickness of love is incurable." Yet the lines have that ineluctable virtue of lightness that Andrei Sinyavsky identified as a facet of that greatness in Pushkin which a reader sometimes feels but is at a loss to describe. The standard Persian rose and nightingale (*gol ō bolbol*) undergo Christianization

Zvart finished, and looked at the monks: the whites of their eyes were bared against him like gleaming knives.

(28) Azaria, sputtering with jealousy, stepped forward, opened his bitter mouth, and began to spew accusations:

"These words about the flower are of the body and of the love of this world."

"His words are filthy," murmured the other monks.

"Don't condemn him. The boy's thoughts are pure!"

But Azaria had thrown off bridle and rein, and pressed ahead, neck straining free: "He is possessed by demons. It is necessary to kill him and the demon within him!" he screamed, his voice thick with bitterness – and he charged Zvart like an enraged bull.

"Stand back, spawn of darkness!" The abbot raised his hand. "By what right do you slay one who is without sin?"

But the abbot was disturbed. The agitation had caught fire at last, and he had to save the boy from these furious fanatics. What should he do? He looked confidently at Zvart.

"Can you recite words of exegesis?" demanded the abbot in severe tones.

Zvart discerned the alarm in the other's soul, wandered for a moment through the world of his thoughts, and returned, taut and confident. And he began:

(29) Shall I say who the red rose is
Or who all the flowers are,
Or who is the nightingale brave,
Or what is the nightingale's voice?

The flowers are the priests of the old Law; the Rose, Jesus; the violet, Judas who betrayed Him; and the nightingale is Gabriel, the trumpeter. The Rose who put on the purple is Christ, who rose

---

and are commonly in Armenian poetry Christ and St. John the Baptist, though here the bird becomes Gabriel. The green leaf as shroud is a nice and complex touch: the Persian poet Ḥāfez asks for the green leaf as his shroud (*kafan*, cf. Arm. *kapan*, both Iranian) and the minstrel (*moṭreb*) to sing over his grave. The green leaf (*barg-e sabz*), sign of burgeoning spring and the poet's gift, mocks death; and the greater life, the Rose, reverses the reversal and to Him even the leaf is but a white shroud.

from the dead; and the flowers who wilted and turned yellow are soldiers who fled from His tomb.

The abbot listened with satisfaction – the monks were dumbstruck. Zvart had won. But Azaria detected a mischievous sparkle in Zvart's eyes, the clever game of a crafty mind. He felt that Zvart's thought was of the "corporeal" kind. But his dull wits could not blossom with the art to contradict. He went dark, like a cave, and retreated. The others went away, too.

After that, for a whole day, the cells resounded with the bitter sound of curses. The abbot was straitened. He felt the end of everything. One night he wrote for a long time in the continuation of his book. He was writing his last will and testament. He had become embittered by the accusatory, envious harrassment. In his testament, he castigated human (30) ignorance and praised the truth.

"Let my body turn to nothing like smoke – my thoughts of truth remain. You will steal my body and scatter its members like chaff, but my thought will endure like the light of the sun. Do not touch me, children of darkness (he threatened in his will) – I am truth and I will exact revenge from you."

He wrote late into the night. At dawn he woke Zvart and Lucian, called them to his side, kissed them, and told them he was going.

"Where?" asked Lucian – but at once he understood and burst into bitter sobs. The abbot entrusted his sacred book to the boys and bade them guard it well. And he died.

They buried the abbot with the respect they were compelled to display, but in profound hatred.

Lucian secretly conveyed the book to Thaddeus, and they buried it in a secret receptacle of stone.

The next day the monks shut Zvart within a dark, tiny cell and forbade him to sing his song of the flowers. Only Lucian visited him. Zvart stared at him in grief and began to speak, to recite his epic ode. Lucian listened, listened, and both forgot they were in a (31) prison. Lucian loved to hear the ode.

brush. The youths turned to stone. The parchment smiled, in sacred silence.

A book of golden fire, full of lights and wisdom. Flaming bird-animals, fish-beasts, and flowers framed two epics. One speaks of the architectonic principle of the universe and the sanctity of the builder's labor; while the other, which flows from page to page like a burning ribbon, is Zvart's epic about flowers.

(36) Snow falls like light. But the monastery is black, and the nook is dark, where a book is imprisoned with the other manuscripts and is being destroyed by damp. They say it is always like this: parchments are ruined by damp. There are flowers in that book. Have the flowers gone to sleep in the book, or are they, too, perishing?

The monastics live to swell their bellies. They have puffed up like toads and have forgotten Zvart, the abbot, Thaddeus and his disciples. They have thrown them all out of the monastery and now they are scattered God knows where.

(37) Night. A winter storm. There is a storm in the mountains of Armenia. It is cold, the sky is frozen glass. Lucian trudges over the ridges, a pouch at his waist, a musty silk pouch in his hand. His stiffened fingers are blue but his fingers are nailed like iron to the binding of the book, which stings with cold beneath the silk. His fingers will freeze solid, but he will not let the book drop from his hand. He has fled the hermitage. He only knows one thing: he is liberating books. Let them but be freed... He does not know himself where he is going. This is a world-destroying snowstorm in the alpine land. Armies course through the valleys. Cities, villages, monasteries, and libraries are burning.

(38) By daybreak the squall had emptied out all its fury over the mountains and plains. At the door of a dilapidated mountain abbey, which an old monk had opened, a man appeared, half-buried in snow, with a pack at his waist and in his hand a book tangled in silk, which had opened and was smiling at the blue heavens.

The old monk looked at the book and, trembling, took it.

(39) A dark cloud obscures the book and its history. A century of a history. Nothing else appears. Only a small opening allows a glimpse at a fragment.

The roads clang beneath the hooves of Sultan Yildirim's cavalry.[27]

He courses past, swift as the cloud of a hailstorm. The earth is tongue-tied, only Yildirim is to be heard.

In a monastery cell an elderly man is seated, immersed in the study of books. He is deaf to the terror. He reads. Two soldiers enter. He does not regard them. They shout. He does not heed. The soldiers are enraged and shoot the old man with arrows. He falls.

Shortly thereafter, fire began to lick at the books, heavy, bitter, acrid like a swarm of flies. The parchments crackle. The soldiers warm themselves and the cracking sound (40) amuses them. Once they were rested and sated, they looked all around and noticed the old man. They stared with innocent, frightened eyes: they feel they were wrong to kill him.

"What sort of books are these?"

"Who knows?"

"They say a book gets angry, brings punishment... The truth is written in them." (Poor soldier, in a book alone, or also within oneself?)

Suddenly a book burst and flew aside from the fire. Was it not touched? Parchment, oil, fire... But they were shaken, and, falling on the fire, put it out. The books began, heavily, bitterly, to smoulder.

They fled outside, to the road.

"The book was angry."

"Yes, one cannot burn the book."[28]

---

[27]Tk. *Yildirim*, "Lightning", was the nickname of Sultan Bayazid I, who conquered central Asia Minor for the Ottomans and who was defeated in turn by Tamerlane in 1402 near Ankara: the historian T'ovma Mecop'ec'i is the principal Armenian source for this period.

[28]*Ayo, girk'ə č'i kareli vaŕel*. Mikhail Bulgakov finished the first draft of his novel *The Master and Margarita* in 1936 and kept working on it through the summer of 1938. He read parts to friends, but the novel – and then only in a censored form – was not to be printed till a quarter century after his death in 1940. The Master is the author of a novel on Pontius Pilate which the Soviet

(41) The willows soughed in the vale, paused to think, and soughed again. Then like a chill river autumn flowed down from the ridges to the valley floor. A new rushing sound was added to the soughing: it was the mossy water of the watermill trap: Jacob the miller was letting it out. No point in letting it down the channels to move the wheel.

---

literary establishment attacks so bitterly that he burns the manuscript. His lover Margarita intercedes with Woland – Mephistopheles come to 1930s Moscow – and the Prince of Darkness returns the book, magically, to its author: "'Let me have a look at it.' Woland extended an upturned palm. 'I am afraid I am unable to do that,' replied the master, 'because I burnt it in the stove.' 'Pardon, I cannot believe that,' answered Woland. 'It is impossible. Manuscripts do not burn (*rukopisi ne goryat*).' He turned to Behemoth and said, 'Well, Behemoth, let me have the novel.' The cat jumped instantly from the chair, and everybody saw he had been seated atop a thick package of manuscripts. The cat handed Woland the top copy with a bow." (Mikhail Afanas'evich Bulgakov, *Master i Margarita, Sobranie sochinenii*, t. 8, Ann Arbor: Ardis, 1988, st. 287, translation mine.) The phrase "manuscripts do not burn" has become proverbial in Russian to express defiance against the destroyers of culture and faith in the miraculous survival of art against the odds. That faith was uncannily vindicated: the Soviet secret police themselves had kept diaries of Bulgakov's thought to have been destroyed and lost, and they were published in 1990 (see J.A.E. Curtis, *Manuscripts Don't Burn: Mikhail Bulgakov, A Life in Letters and Diaries*, Woodstock, NY: Overlook Press, 1992, pp. xii, 225). Many books were burnt in the Soviet Union in the Great Terror – the years when Bulgakov was finishing his great work. I have in my library a copy of the banned *Girk' Čanaparhi*, "The Book of the Journey," by the Armenian poet Yeghishe Charents, that barely escaped the flames (see J.R. Russell, "The Armenian Counterculture That Never Was: Reflections on Eghishe Charents," *Journal of the Society for Armenian Studies* 9, 1996-97 (1999), pp. 17-35). Its author was murdered in 1937. Demirjian is unlikely to have heard of Bulgakov's work on his novel when "The Book of Flowers" was written, so it is safe to suggest that his line independently, originally, anticipates Bulgakov's. And there is no evidence at all to suggest Bulgakov knew of Demirjian's story. Life in the same country, it would seem, inspired reactions uncannily similar from two writers in very different regions of it.

There was famine throughout the land.

Jacob took counsel with his young son beneath the willow.

"Go to Damascus, Husik. They've set up mills there. Go bring grain, we'll plant it. Our livelihood won't perish." Husik's blue eyes smiled, full of sorrow. He repeated:

(42) "Livelihood!" and laughed aloud, looking at his father.

"What sort of foolishness are you listening to? Come to your senses, the land is being destroyed."

Jacob went into the watermill house, extracted a flowered robe from a corner, five silk handkerchiefs, and then with his leathery fingers groped and pulled from a pouch thirty ducats.[29] "I made ten ditches – that's the price. You'll sell the robe to cover expenses on the road, you'll do some odd jobs, bring some home, and by spring we'll throw something into the soil's mouth. Our livelihood won't perish."

Husik looks at his father's eyes. His father affects him the way nature does. He is saying something profound, some sort of frightening thing.

Husik took the road towards Damascus.

Husik walks with a blue, sad smile in his eyes. The distant blue of a distant fatherland.

Sunburnt roads traverse the land. They carry saddlebags full of fragrant smells: dates, grain, tobacco,[30] coffee.

Husik walks along, seeming to glide over the world, thinking. And he smiles in his mischievous way. "What was Dad saying about our livelihood not perishing?" Who or what will save a man? The land? They'll take it away. The Amira, with his soldiers?

(43) The princes of the Seljuks and Tatars are arrayed against him, and, like flood crashing against flood, they devour and devastate each other. Wealth, maybe – but Husik had seen how the rich

---

[29]*Dahekan*, literally a gold daric. In Ottoman times, Armenians used the word to mean one hundredth of a gold *oski* (Malxaseanc', s.v.).

[30]*P'stoc'*, a rather uncommon word, the more usual one for tobacco being *t'ut'un* (see J.R. Russell, "The Demon Weed," forthcoming in the *Journal of Armenian Studies*, a translation and study of a late mediaeval Armenian poem lamenting the evils of tobacco and tracing it back to the Egyptian magicians Jannes and Jambres). Nowadays tobacco is called *cxaxot* /dzekhakhot/, "smoke-grass."

were stripped naked, the gold went, and skeletons remained. So, what will save life, what is a way of life's bedrock?

The bedrock – that is what Husik's mind sought. And Husik, burning with sweat, trembled like a desiccated prickly pear in the yellow sea of the sun.

"Oh, if a man could become a bird and take away with him in his flight gold, bread, clothes, life! But what's the use, kites and eagles in the sky would rend the man and pillage everything he had."

The gold-dusted city was ablaze with sunlight. A surging multitude boiled through it. Husik's eyes darted, bedazzled. Here is a fiery youth, his bronze arms in the air, twisting a sparkling sword. The steel jerks and straightens like a serpent. Bronze young men surround him and laugh with their pearly teeth. Camels kneel around the plane trees, packs of grain and all sorts of other goods piled haphazardly to either side of each.

He sat down among the saddlebags, resting his back against the treetrunk. The sun scorches him, the heat suffocates him. He looks at the houses enclosing the marketplace, at (44) the people, all burnt by the hot sun. Billowing waves of blue water rolled in, in Husik's eyes. He even felt their icy kiss upon his parched lips. Sleep approached his eyes. He cast about a hazy look. Did he stare long, had he fallen asleep and awakened – he didn't remember. He looked up and now saw a motley crowd in front of him who were laughing, passing from hand to hand, and roughly opening and shutting a book with their tawny fingers. Husik got up, captivated by something familiar. What is it? Yes, the appearance of the book. He has seen books of this sort. He came closer. Another hand seized the book – and he himself began to explore its black leather and silver casing. Then he opened the book and looked at the pages.

Springs and fruit-ripened autumns opened, ruby skies, herb gardens, roses of fire, tigers of molten gold and meandering blossoms, warm, entranced, ecstatic. The intimate colors of his own mountains and valleys formed pictures in Husik's eyes.

What was written in this book, that was so passionately illuminated? They were selling the book. The seller was an Arab soldier, kind-faced and carefree. He had acquired the item during an an invasion and had been so stupid as to bring it all the way to Damascus. "What was the point?"

"Hmm ... what should I pay?" says a man, twisting his mouth in a laugh.

(45) "Thirty ducats."

The buyer snorted and the book flew, landed on the ground in the dust. The others kicked it around. The soldier laughed, went over and lazily picked up the book and held it. He was having a good time selling it and finding no customers.

Husik went up and touched the book. The silver was warm beneath his fingers. He opened the book. He looked at it lightly, calmly. Eyes appeared from the midst of the flowers. The scent of a vernal wisdom, an enduring life wafted from them. The book was as placid as a man who knows all life's laws and the secret of a way of life and does not fear death, loves life and has faith in the face of destiny. Husik read, declaiming, "For labor is holy."

Husik remembered, only now, his cheerful, wine-loving great-grandfather Sargis, of whom they said that he had been a vigorous mason. He used to sing while he labored: he sang even in days of disaster, and never aged. Once, when he was coming home from work, he saw that burglars had robbed his house. The family were stripped stark naked. But great-grandfather Sargis had just caw-cawed with laughter.

"They haven't stolen my hands."

(46) In the leanest days he used to say, "We'll work, and we'll live."

That is what he had said to his son, a famous builder, and he to his, and the latter to his own son, Husik's father. So his father had heard, and his father before him from his father, that the greatest thing in the world is labor.

"Labor is holy." That's how it was written in the book, that's what Husik's forebears used to say – workers, all of them. He read again, "For labors are holy." Could this be that book, then? Husik's eyes were on fire, and his thought lost itself in the distance.

He took out his money and handed it to the soldier. The latter pocketed it and briskly shoved the book into Husik's hands. Then he walked off, laughing. The others laughed after him, and stared incredulously at Husik.

He was dreaming.

Some other strange men came over, looked at the book, at Husik. And as he was about to put the book in his bag, a familiar voice startled him. It was Solomon, his countryman.

"Are you crazy, or just a fool? You gave your money for that book?"

"Yes." Husik looked at Solomon with his crooked, slightly stupid smile.

(47) "So what are you going to plant in the springtime, then?" Husik stared dumbly and a spark of sadness twinkled for a moment in his eyes.

Was he confused, or was he playing some kind of joke? "Let's go home now, you idiot."

He will go home and famine will have settled there. An ashen vortex engulfs the book, and nothing more can be seen.

What became of Husik? How did he survive the hunger – that is, the death? Crazy, crazy Husik...

In the book's colophon[31] it is inscribed how he paid his money for the book ... thinking, as it seems, that not even grain was life, that not even that could save life from death.

(48) From beneath a sick child's pillow (centuries have passed, again, though they have moved with a terrific, heavy slowness) that book peeps out, in hope of life. Nobody in this illiterate farming family knows what sort of book it is. They found it in the ashes of a ruined house. They say it cures every illness. The child has a disease of the soul...

(49) What caravan is this? Where are you headed now, Hoja?"[32]
"Venice, Genoa, wherever good fortune leads."

---

[31] Arm. *yišatakaran*, literally "container of memorials." These are a particularly rich primary source for Armenian history, containing the names of scribes, painters, donors, receivers, and their families, with abundant information about the conditions and events of the time. See Avedis K. Sanjian, *Colophons of Armenian Manuscripts, 1301-1480*, Cambridge, MA: Harvard University Press, 1969.

[32] Perso-Turkish *khwāja*, "Master."

The Hoja is bent over, absorbed in reading, by the side of the endless, sun-baked road. In the camels' packs are red dye, madder, leather, gemstones. The caravan rests. The camels are grazing.

The Hoja reads and chases away the melancholy of the journey.

(50) A book emerges out of the black ages. Like a light wandering through the darkness, it wavers, but it comes. It cannot see what dangers it is passing through – neither winter, nor dark. Fire doesn't burn it, heat cannot suffocate it. Is it miracle that protects it, or mere chance? But the generations look after it, hide it, rescue it, and bequeath it to their heirs, passing it down from hand to hand through the tribulations of the centuries, passing it across fire and water and the sword.

The book smiles. Is it simple, or carefree, or crafty? Does it know how to manage its affairs? Or is it wise, and aware of the writing on its path?

(51) Like the sunlight, that plays, carefree, on the foam of the ferocious breakers of the ocean. The waves gleam yellow and blue, erupt in spume, roar and shake their fists at the sun, but it smiles. It knows no peril or hatred – these do not touch it, the wave does not shatter it.

A thousand hands have kept, caressed, touched these flowers, this beauty of life, and thousands upon thousands of eyes have looked at them in love and sorrow as they passed. A thousand hands have turned to dust, a thousand eyes full of passion, and this warm book has remained.

(52) An entire people is being exterminated. Never mind a book. The mighty cannons predict: "It is lost!" No. "It's saved!" "It would be a miracle if it survived..."

(53) A stormy red wind[33] turns the pages of golden light of a book which is on a great road, upon which it gazes with familiarity. It has been saved, with the nation that always saves it.

---

[33] This is undoubtedly a metaphor of the red banner of the October Revolution and the establishment of Soviet rule in Armenia.

In iron libraries the centuries are silent. A grey head is bent over the abyss of history, and in a deep valley he sees: flowers, flowers, flowers!...

ԴԵՐԵՆԻԿ ԴԵՄԻՐՃՅԱՆ

ԳԻՐՔ ԾԱՂԿԱՆՑ

«Սովետական գրող» Հրատարակչություն
Երևան — 1985

ԳՄԴ 84 Հ7
Դ 353

Նկարիչ՝
ԱԲԵՐՏ ԿԱՐԱԳՅԱՆ

Դեմիրճյան, Դ.

Դ 353 Գիրք ծաղկանց։ Պատմվածք /Նկ.՝ Ա. Կարագյան. — Եր.: Սովետ. գրող, 1985. — 56 էջ.

Դերենիկ Դեմիրճյանի այս պատմվածքը հայ արձակի գլուխգործոցներից է, լավագույն գեղարվեստական երկը՝ նվիրված հայ հին մանրանկարչությանը։

Դ $\frac{4702080200 (66)}{705 (01) 85}$ 85 «Տ»

ԳՄԴ 84 Հ7

© «Սովետական գրող» հրատարակչություն, ձևավորման համար, 1985

Մաշի ձեռս, դառնա ի հող,
Գիրս մնա հիշատակող:
(Միջնադարյան)

 աղիկները կրակներ են, պտուղներն ազ-
նիվ քարեր,— նա այդպես էր տեսնում,—
իսկ թռչուններն ու գազանները զգես-
տավորված խեղկատակներ, խաղում են առակներ թա-
գավորների, իշխանների, գյուղացիների կյանքից, այն,
որ պատմել է իր տատիկը։ Նրա համար քարափները
խռոված նայում են, իսկ լեռներն ալիքներ են փո-
թորկված Վանա ծովի:

— Տեսեք,— մին էլ ասում էր նա,— պատանին առ-
յուծին նստած գնում է:

— Ո՞ւր է... Ո՞ւր է,— հետաքրքիր վրա էին վազում
խաղընկերները:

Ցույց էր տալիս Ջվարթը դաշտի քարակույտերը և ծիծաղելով վազում էր, գնում փողոցն ի վար։

Նայում էին և ոչինչ չէին տեսնում դաշտի քարակույտերում։ Եվ հետևից էին ընկնում, որ ծեծեն Ջվարթին խաբելու համար։ Բայց նրան հասնում էին բլրի վրա մի ծաղկի գլխի կռացած։ Ու մինչ պատրաստվում էին խփել նրան, նա թավիշէ ծաղիկը ձեռքը վերցնելով ծիծաղում ու ցույց էր տալիս.

— Վարդապետը, վարդապետը, գլխին վեղար՝ կուն- ձիկ-մունձիկ գնում է վանք։

Ու կոմիկ շարժումներով տիկնիկի խաղ էր սարքում, տմբտմբացնում ծաղկի գլուխը, փայլեցնում ձեռքի վրա։ Երեխաները ծեծը մոռացած ծիծաղում էին և հետո էլ զարմանքով նայում նրան։

— Ի՞նչ տեսակ տղա է...

Պատահում էր՝ նստում էին քարափին։ Արդեն Ջվարթը պատմում էր.

— Գնացել էի ձորը, գետի ափը։ Փրփուրների միջին մի աղջիկ ինձ փսփսաց. «Արի, Ջվարթ, արի, արի»։ Գնացի, ինձ տարավ հեռու, գետի տակը։ Պալատներ կային, նախշուն քարերով, մարգարիտներով...

— Սուտ ես խոսում, — գոչում էր ընկերներից մինը, բամփում գլխին, և երեխաները կրկին հարձակվում էին վրան խփելու, բայց Ջվարթը փախչում էր տուն։ Հետևից քար էին նետում։

Իսկ տանը ծնողներին ու հարևաններին արդեն պատմում էր, որ ձորի միջով ուկե ուղտեր անցան. մեկ ուղտի վրա կապիկ էր նստած ակնեղեն աթաղաղը ձեռքին, իսկ մյուսը՝ նառը* հագել էր ոսկեթել շուրջառ, նրա մեջքին էլ վարդն էր նստել, որի դեմքը լուսին էր՝ շրջանակած վարդի կրակե թերթերով։

Ծնողներն ու հարևանները լսում են, իրար նայում նշանակալից և տխուր։ Նրանցից մինը գլուխն օրորում է.

— Աստծուց գտնես փրկություն, զավակս։

Երեկոն մանիշակ ցանեց գյուղի, դիմացի քարափների ու անդնդի այգիների վրա։ Հետո, երբ Ձվարթը քնած էր, հարևան պառավ Սանդուխտը դեմքը մոտեցրեց Ձվարթի մորը։

— Շեն տիկին, տղադ ցավագա՞ր է, չարո՞ց է։

Իսկ հարևան ձերունի Գաղիշոն, խստադեմ, սրբակ-յաց մի մարդ՝ մարգարեական անհակառակելի խոսքով կտրում է.

— Ընձայեցե՛ք սուրբ Նշանին։

Ձվարթի մայրը տխրեց։ Հայրը մռայլվեց։

Ու հստակ այդ երեկոյին, մի հազարամյակ առաջ, երբ հարազատ ձորիդը մտերմաբար ձորում էր պատի ձեղքում, Ձվարթի ծնողները վճռեցին նրան տանել սուրբ Նշան վանքին ընձայելու։

---

* Քարավանի առաջից գնացող ուղտը։

Գարունը հնում է Հայաստանի լեռնաշխարհում։ Օրը չինչ, աղբյուրը կոհակում է խաղաղ։ Զվարթենք, նրանց գյուղացիներն ուխտ են գնում լեռան մի վանք։ Գնում են շարան շարքերով, սայլերի վրա, հետևակ։ Նստել է սայլին Զվարթը և դիտում է գյուղացիների նոր զգեստները և նրանցից մեկը նրան թվում է վագրենի հագած։ Ու ծիծաղում է վրան. «Ո՛ր կերթաս, Չելեբի, վագր ես դառել, Չելեբի»։

Ու զնգում է նրա ծիծաղը։
«Չելեբին» սառը նայում է Զվարթի հորը և գլուխն օրորում։ Իսկ մայրն աչքերն է սրբում։ Զվարթը սողաց դեպի լուծը, որ նստի սայլի գլխին, քեռի Մանուկի մոտ։ Քեռի Մանուկը գրկեց Զվարթին և ճիպոտը տվեց ձեռը։ Զվարթն սկսեց քշել եզներին։ Հետո հանկարծ մատն ուղղեց եզան աչքի մեջ և ցույց տվեց քեռի Մանուկին։
— Քեռի՛, քեռի՛, տե՛ս։
— Ի՞նչ է, ճագուկ։
— Տե՛ս, եզան աչքի մեջ գիշեր է։— Քեռի Մանուկը ծիծաղում է։
Սայլն ընկավ մի մարմանդ հովիտ ու սկսեց սուրալ։ Քեռի Մանուկը երգեց.
Աստղի ի՛ ի՛ կ մը յերկնուց ի վա՛մ ա՛ մ ր կու սիրե ձկնակն ի
ծովունուն...
Ո՛, ո՛չ աստղիկն է ի վամր գալու ո՛, ո՛չ ձկնակն ի վեեր գնալու...

8

Լսում է Չվարթը, և նրա աչքերը գոհարների պես ցոլում են հետաքրքրությունից.
— Քեռի, աստղիկը ճկնակին շա՞տ կու սիրէ։
— Շա՛տ, — ճգում է քեռի Մանուկն ու հառաչում։
— Քեռի, ապա իսկի չպիտո՞ իջնա աստղիկը ճկնակին քով։
— Չէ, ճագուկ, չէ, — հառաչում է քեռի Մանուկը։
— Հեռո՞ւ է երկինքը։
— Հեռու՜ն...

Չվարթը խորասուզվում է մտքերի ծովը, թե ինչու ճկնակն ինքը չի գնում երկինք։ Բայց այդ միջոցին նրա ուշքը գրավում է գետակը, որ հովի վրա իր կոհակները շողալելով, ասեղնագործում է տասնյակ ժապավեններ։ Իսկ երկու կողմում՝ ժայռերից ծիլ-ծիլ հյուսվում են լուսեղեն աղբյուրներ։

Թերակողջի, երկու կողմն անդունդ։ Սսավոր մի վանք նայում է այնտեղից խիստ ու գեղեցիկ։ Երկինք է միտում նրա գմբեթը նետադեղի պես լարված։ Նրա շուրջն են խոնվել ուխտավորները։

Հանկարծ Չվարթը մատը մեկնեց վանքի պատին և դրդեց հորը.
— Հայրի՛, հայրի՛, տես ծառի տակին ո՞վ է կանգնած նուռը ձեռին։
— Որտե՞ղ...

— Պատի վրա,— Զվարթը հետաքրքիր նայում է պատին:

Հայրը, ուխտավորները զարմանքով ու ցավով նայում են վանքի պատին: Այնտեղ ոչինչ չկա: Վանքն է բարձրաշեն ու սրբատաշ: Ծեղքվածքների գծեր են խաղում պատի վրա: Զվարթը մարդ է տեսնում այդ գծերում և գվարճացած ծիծաղում:

— Ա՛յ, ա՛յ, աչքերի վրա աղեղակներ...

Բայց շրջապատողները վախեցած են արդեն: Հավաքվեցին մյուս ուխտավորները և երկյուղած նայեցին Զվարթին, որ աշխույժ մատով օդում կրկնում է գծերը:

— Նուռը տալիս է եղնիկին: Տեսեք եղջյուրները:

Ուխտավորները երեսները խաչակնքում են: Զվարթի մայրն արտասվում է, իսկ հայրը խիստ ազդված, դողահար, բռնում է Զվարթի ձեռը: Վանահայրն է միայն, որ գոհունակ նայում է Զվարթին:

Զվարթենց հարկանը փսփսում է վանահոր ականջին:

— Աչքին մի՞շտ կեռնան, հայր սուրբ, ո՞նց որ երազ:

— Շնորհաց աղբյուրին ապավեն լինենք,— մրմնջում է վանահայրը:

Հարկանները, համագյուղացիները սրտերն առնված նայում են Զվարթին և ափսոսում նրան: Զվարթը պիտի մնա վանքում, նվիրվի վանքին: Նա էլ չի տեսնելու իրենց տունը:

Ժամերգությունն սկսվեց։ Խորին անդնդից ասես ուղտերի զանգեր եղանակեցին, որոնց արձագանքը դղանձեց ներսից։ Ուխտավորները, բացի կանանցից, մտան սրբավայրը։

Սևացած, փոշոտ կամարները թույլ արծիվների պես թևաբաց իջնում են վերևից։ Անկյուններում արդեն մթնում են ստվերները։ Կանթեղը թույլ դողում է բեմի խորքում, մշուշի մեջ լողացող աստղի պես։ Սևազգեստ վանականները կոկորդախայն կոնչում են ինչ-որ աղոթքներ։ Եվ անկյունները տխուր են, տխուր` մեռելի փակված աչքերի նման։

Ճնշվում է Ջվարթի հոգին։ Նա երկյուղով նայում է հատակին, չի համարձակվում աչքը վեր բարձրացնել։

Ժամերգությունը վերջացավ։ Ջվարթին տարան բեմ, մոտեցրին մի ահավոր հանգուցյալի, որի դեմքը կաշվե դիմակ էր, որը մեռելի մեռած մորուք ուներ և ոսկրե ձեռներ։ Նրա այտը և մի աչքի տակն այրված էր մոմից։ Նա շրջանակի միջից ահռելի նայում էր Ջվարթին։ Ջվարթին մոտ տարան դեպի մեռելը։

— Համբուրե՛, համբուրե՛,— շշնջացին հետևից նրան։

...Ջրերի կոհակներն են խշխշում, խշխշում են երկար, հեռվից, խորքից։ Մի մեծ ձուկ լաց է լինում, «Ո՛չ, վո՛ւչ, Ջվա՛րթ, տղա՛ս, վո՛ւչ»։

Բաց է անում աչքերը Ջվարթը,— ի՞նչ է, ու՞ր է... Նրա գլխավերևն նստած է հայրը, կողքին մայրը, որ ծնկներին է ծեծում։ Մի կողմում շարված են ուխտավորները, իսկ ոտների մոտ նստած է մի մարմարե ճերունի, որը հանգիստ նայում է Ջվարթին և այդ հայացքով նա նման է, այ, հենգ այն ճերունի ամպին, որ երկնակապույտի մեջ կորամեջք գնում է ուր որ։

Իրիկնադեմին Ջվարթենք և բոլոր ուխտավորները քաշվեցին։ Ամենքը գնացին, մնաց մթնած դաշտը, խավարած վանքը, սառնածոր աստղերը երկնքում։ Անճուկ դառավ վանքի բակը, լռեց գերեզմանաքարի պես և նրա մեջ թաղված աշխույժ թիթեռը — փոքրիկ Ջվարթը։

Հեռուն, հեռուն, որտեղ գնացին Ջվարթենք և գյուղացիները, հովիտը լցված է փիրուզե մշուշով։ Դա հայրենիքի ճանապարհն է։ Ջվարթը տխուր նայեց այն կողմ և սրտաբեկ հառաչեց։ Վանահոր փոքրավորը նրան տարավ վանահոր խուցը, ուր նա կօկվեց մի ոչխարենու վրա։ Վանահայրը նստեց ճիթածրագի լույսի առջև, վերցրեց մի սևակազի գիրք և խոշոր աչքերը գրքին հառած, սկսեց կիսաձայն մրմնջալ։ Նա ծովի էր նման, օտար ու մշուշոտ։ Ջվարթը նայում էր նրան և գրքին։ Վանահայրը կախ էր գցել նրա մի էջը, և երևում էր այդ էջի վրա մի ոսկեշող կամար, կապույտ սյուներ և ծաղիկներ։ Ջվարթը տխրեց, երբ տեսավ ծաղիկները։ Դա հիշեցրեց նրան իրենց դաշտերի ու ձորերի ծաղիկները։ Հանկարծ ճրագի լույսը, ճերունին, գիրքը, բոլորը բեկ-

բեկվեցին արտասուքի կաթիլի մեջ, որ բխեցին Զվարթի աչքից։ Նա սկսեց հեկեկալ։ Ինչու՞ բերին իրեն, թողին այս լռին ու օտար վայրում։ Ե՞րբ պիտի տանեն իրեն։ Այլևս չի տեսնելու ծնողներին, ընկերներին։ Իրեն․ թողեցին ու գնացին։ Ամբողջ սրտով լաց եղավ։ Գիշերը տաքություն եկավ վրան։ Տենդի մեջ սկսեց այլվել։ Ջրեր սկսեցին խշշալ նրա ականջներում, ծաղիկների մի հեղեղ եկավ խռնվեց նրա աչքերում։ Չոր շրթունքները թացում էր ջրերի մեջ, խմում անհագ ու որքան խմում էր, այնքան ծարավն այրում էր իրեն։ Մի քանի օր ոչինչ չէր գիտակցում։ Սիայն մի ճերմակ ճմեռ-վանահայրը լցվում էր խուցն ու գրվում հետո։ Ծերունին նայում էր նրան հանդարտ ու սպասում։

Եվ մի օր Զվարթը աչքերը բացեց։ Մառը քրտինքը ճակատին նա հանգիստ շունչ քաշեց։ Նա ապաքինված էր։ Փոքրավորը նրան ապուր բերեց ու աղբյուրի սառնորակ ջուր։

Զվարթն ապաքինվեց, բայց և սկսեց գաղտնի մաշ-վել։ Հայրենիքի բույրերը հովի ու ծաղիկների հետ գալիս լցվում էին վանքի գավիթը և նրան քաշում հեռավոր տուն, խաղընկերների մոտ։ Մթնակապույտ հեռանում էին լեռները դեպի այդ տունը, ծիծեռնակները սլանում էին այն կողմ, լողում ամպերը, որ կարապներ էին վրան ճերմակ աղջիկներ հեծած։ Նստում էր պարսպի տակ, անդնդի եզրին Զվարթը և նայում դեպի իրենց տան կողմը, լեռներն ու դաշտերը: Մտերմաբար իջնում էր երեկոն, շոյում նրա վառվող այքերը և Դունկիանոսը փոքրավորը նրան գտնում էր քնած անդնդի եզրին: Զարթնեցնում էր և տանում խուցը:

Իսկ ձմեռը՝ ձյան փաթիլներն աղավնիների պես ճախրում էին անդնդի վրա, և Զվարթը մտքով նրանց հետ խաղում էր, խաղում և հետո գալիս մտնում խուցը, ոչխարենու մեջ կծկվում, քնում:

Փոքրավոր Դունկիանոսը, մի խեղճ ու կրակ երիտասարդ էր, բայց անսահման բարի, որ շատ խղճաց Զվարթին և կապվեց նրա հետ: Վանականների սառ հայացքներից սիրտը պաղած, Զվարթը նրան էր որոնում: Դունկիանոսի մեջ ջերմություն կար, կյանքի նշույլ: Նա էր միայն, որ սիրտ էր տալիս Զվարթին:

Նա Զվարթին սիրում էր կարծես: Այնուհետև ոչխարենու վրա պառկած Զվարթը հանգիստ էր դիտում ծերունի վանահորը, որ անքուն, անդադար գրում էր մագաղաթի վրա: Ի՞նչ էր գրում նա, ի՞նչ մտքերի մեջ էր խորասուզվում այդ խորին ծերունին: Զվարթի մտքերը թափառում էին այդ ծերունու շուրջը, կորչում, կրկին դառնում նրան: Տարօրինակ մարդ էր վանահայրը: Նա, այդ ինքնամփոփ, խոր մարդը վերին աստիճան հետաքրքրում էր Զվարթին: Ո՞վ էր նա իսկապես: Դունկիանոսը լսել էր և պատմում էր Զվարթին: Վանահայրը նախկին ճարտարապետ է և փիլիսոփա: Նա կառուցել է

14

վանքեր, լսարաններ ու պարիսպներ։ Այժմ, երբ մարմնական ուժը պակասել է, մտել է վանք փիլիսոփայությամբ զբաղվելու։ Նրան աբեղաները չեն հարգում, քանի որ նա հոգևոր տենչով չի եկել վանք, նա «հոգևորաց» չէ, «մարմնավորաց» է։

Ի՞նչ է նշանակում այս։ Ջվարթն ավելի է վառվում հետաքրքրությամբ, ո՞ր հասկանա այդ մարդուն։ Եվ ուսուցման ժամերին, երբ նա ու Ղունկիանոսը ծալապատիկ նստած էին լինում վանահոր դիմաց՝ Ջվարթն աչքերը լայն բացած, ուշակորույս ունկնդրում էր այդ անհուն մարդուն։ Միայն դեռ լավ չէ ըմբռնում նրա նորօրինակ, անլուր մտքերը։ Նա միայն տեսնում էր իր առջև ծովի նման խորը մի էակի, որ խոսում է, խոսում է հենց ծովի պես, որին լսում ես անհագ տենչով, բայց չես հասկանում որի լեզուն։ Ջվարթն զգում էր ինչ-որ արբեցնող վերասլացումն։

Խցից դուրս, բնության անհուն դահլիճում շքեղ հանդես է։ Վառվում է երկնային ջահը, և լեռներն ու անդունդները շքեղանում են հանդիսավոր լույսով։ Թռչունները սրտապատառ ցնծությամբ ճախրում են օդում։ Աշխարհը տոնում է ամենավսեմ բանը՝ կյանքը և նրա ուրախությունը։

Վանահայրը նստած է խցում, համրիչը քաշում փիլիսոփայորեն։ Ջվարթն ու Ղունկիանոսը ծունկ-ծնկի ծալապատիկ նստած՝ սերտում են ինչ-որ հատված։ Մեղուն տզզալով կտրում է լույսի ոսկի սյունը և լցնում խուցը կյանքի ուրախությամբ։

Հանկարծ արևի շողքը մթնեց դռան առջև։ Ղունկիանոսը վեր նայեց և տեսավ դռան առջև մի բարձրահասակ մարդու։ Սա իր սապատավոր մեջքը խոնարհեց դռան կամարի տակ և գանգուր այծամորուքի ծայրը ցցելով ներս, նայեց Զվարթին արծվի հայացքով և խոնարհություն արեց վանահորը։ Ապա տաղանդի գծերով կնքված ձեռքից նրան մի գիրք հրամցրեց. Ղունկիանոսն ու Զվարթը վգները երկարացրին, նայեցին գրքին։ Վանահայրը բացեց գիրքը։ Էջերի վրա բնագրի հետ մեջընդմեջող վանքի ու այլ շենքերի նկարներ կային խստագիծ նկարած, որոնց շուրջը ծաղկած էր։ Արծվաքիթ մարդը, որ, ըստ երևույթին, աշխատել էր այդ գրքի վրա, սկսեց բանալ էջերը և բացատրել։ Զվարթը հասկացավ, որ նա էր զարդարել գիրքը վանահոր համար։

— Գրել է և շենքերը նկարել է հայր սուրբը, իսկ Թադեն արտագրել, ծաղկել է էջերը, — շշնջաց Զվարթի ականջին Ղունկիանոսն անհասկանալի բաներ։

Վանահայրն անդորր նայեց գրքին, հառաչեց և այս աշխարհից հեռացողի երազով նայեց գիրքը ծաղկողին։

— Այժմիկ պատրաստ եմ երթալ առ հարս, Թադե, ահավասիկ վաստակք իմ և կտակ իմ։

Ծաղկողը՝ Թադեն, համբուրեց վանահոր աջը և դուրս գնաց։

Վանահայրը մեղմաժպիտ նայեց Զվարթին ու Ղունկիանոսին և սկսեց բարձրաձայն կարդալ իր հեղինակությունը։ Նա տարվեց իր մտքերով և սկսեց այնպես կարդալ, որ չէր իմացվում, իր համար էր ընթերցումը, թե՞ ուսուցանում էր Զվարթին և Ղունկիանոսին։ — «Կառուցումն է աշխարհն և աշխատք շինողական», — շրջում է գրքի էջը վանահայրը և ոգում, — «Կառուցումն է քաղաքն, կառուցումն խոսքն, կառուցումն միտք»։

Եվ ցույց է տալիս երկինքը, երկիրը, վանքի շենքը, իր ճակատը, իր «միտքը»։ Բացատրում է տիեզերական շինարարության արվեստը։

Զվարթը բոցավառվում է։ Նրա աչքերում գծագրվում և գունավորվում են շքեղ պատկերներ։ Ձնգում են մույթերը և խստադեմ քարտաշները կոփում են ժայռերը, խոհուն որմնադիրներ կանգնեցնում են հոյակապ քաղաքներ երկնասլաց աշտարակներով։ Փարթամ պարտեզներ կախվում են անդունդների վրա։

— «Աշխատ առնե բնությունն, կառուցանե ծառն, շինարարէ մրջյունն։ Եղեք և դուք կառուցողք և շինարարք, որպես մարդիկ երկրի, սիրեցեք աշխատք, զի կառուցումն և աշխատք սուրբ են...»։

— «Զքանա բնություն, փոշիանան գահք և թագավորություն և մնա շինարարն...»։

Խորանում է ծերունին Չվարթի աչքերում։ Այլակերպվում է այդ հրաշքներով լի մարդը։ Նրա մռայլ սքեմը հալվում է և նրա տակից դրսևորվում է «երկրի մարդը», որի միտքն զբաղված է մի մեծ կառուցողական տենչով ու երազով։ Չվարթը խցից դուրս է նայում «աշխարհին»։ Եվ այդ անհուն շենքի մեջ, ուր թռչունները հյուսում են մետաքսե բներ, մրջյունները կառուցում են իրենց բնակարանները, ամբողջ աշխարհը ներկայացնում է որպես մի հսկայական ճարտարապետական կառուցվածք իր երկնքի աշտարակով, նրա վերև կախված արևի ջահով, լեռների սյուներով ու անդունդների նիշերով։

Տանջվում է Չվարթը, գիշերները տապակվում է անքնությունից։ Տանջվում է մի անրմբռնելի տենչից։ Չգիտե որտեղից է գալիս այդ տենչը և ինչ տենչ է դա, որ մեծ է, թե դուրսը, այլ տեղ չգիտե։

Ղունկիանոսը նկատում է նրա տանջանքը և ուզում է օգնել նրան։

— Կարդա՛, Չվա՛րթ, կարդա՛, — սիրտ է տալիս, հորդորում։

Չվարթը նայում է Ղունկիանոսին երազով ու տրխրությամբ։

— Ես անիմա՛ս եմ, Ղունկիանո՛ս, միտքս տկար, երբ պիտի ես էլ իմանամ, թե ի՞նչ եմ։

— Համբերի՛ր, Ջվա՛րթ, կգա տերը շնորհաց, կընդունես շնորհի և միտքդ կկառվի:

— Ի՞նչ բան է շնորհի ընդունելը:

— Շնորհի ընդունելն այն է, որ նա քեզ կասի, թե ի՞նչ ես կամենում և ի՞նչ պիտի անես:

— Ո՞վ է տերը շնորհաց:

Անհասկանալի բաներ է պատմում Ղունկիանոսը, այն, ինչ որ լսել է, բայց ինքն էլ չի հասկացել: Այդ տերը շնորհաց մի լույս է. այսպես է լսել Ղունկիանոսը վանահորից:

— Լո՛ւյս — վախենում է Ջվարթը — չլինի՞ թե գա գիշերը, խավարի մեջ, միայնության ժամին: — Շարունակ անհանգիստ մտածում է այդ եակի մասին:

Շրջում է այդ մտքերով Ջվարթը անդնդի վրա, գառնանային արևը լուսվում է ժայռերի, ծաղիկների, ջրերի վրա և Ջվարթը նրանց արտաքին կերպարանքի տակ, նրանց մեջ բաներ է տեսնում, որ նրանց այլափոխում, դարձնում են շնչավոր, բանական էակներ, որոնց հետ ինքն իր մեջ խոսում է գաղտնի իրենից և գաղտնի լեզվով: Նա նրանց տեսնում է և ամենուրեք, ամպերում, պատերի վրա, խավարի մեջ: Նրանք շարժվում են, մարդու ձևեր ընդունում, խոսում իր հետ, ծիծաղում, կանչում իրեն:

Ջվարթն ակամա, ձեռքով, օդի մեջ գծում էր նրանց պատկերը: Բայց հենց որ մարմնացնում էր նրանց մտովի գծերով, օդի մեջ, նրանք խուսափուկ ու արագ անէանում էին և նրանցից մնում էին ուրիշ բաներ — բառեր, կրակոտ բառեր, որ շշնջում էին նրա ականջին:

Շշնջում, շշնջում և կործում: Հետո կրկին ու կրկին...

Տանջվում է Ձվարթը, տենչում ինչ-որ, ուր-որ...

Բարձրագմբեթ, կամարակապ մի օթևան: Նրա տակին միայնակ կանգնած է Ձվարթը և ունկնդրում լռությանը: Գիշերը ծծումբի աչքերով երկնքից նայում է ներս՝ գողտրիկ պատուհանների արանքով:

Խավար է օթևանում և տխուր: Միայն դուրսը, անդնդում անքուն գետն է վշշում, հովտում տնքում գիշերահավը:

Հանկարծ օթևանի պատը, որը թվում էր անհուն, հեռվից, շատ հեռվից ճեղքվեց և ներս հոսեց ո՜վ — ինքը Ձվարթը... Ձվարթը չի զարմանում: Չէ՞ որ նրան նա տեսել է շատ անգամ՝ աղբյուրների ակունքներում, ցողի մեջ: Նա արեգակնափայլ աչքեր ուներ, որ վառվում էին գոհարների պես: Այդ աչքերն այնպես էին նայում, որ Ձվարթը զարհուրեց: (Իր մեջ աա այդպիսի զարհուրելի բան կա եղել...):

Եվ չիշխեց վեր նայել նրան: Բայց մի ուժ դրդում էր Ձվարթին նայել նրան: Եվ ահա, երբ նա աչքերը վեր բարձրացրեց, զարհուրած ընկավ հատակին: Երկար մնաց այդպես ընկած, հետո ինչ եղավ՝ չի հիշում Ձվարթը:

Միայն զգաց, որ էակը մոտեցավ իրեն և կռանալով ձեռքը դրեց նրա ուսին: Նրա կռանալն զգաց նրանով, որ նա շշնջում էր: Անբացատրելի էր այդ շշունչը, երգածայն, անուշ:

Ջվարքը լսում էր ու օրորվում: Երգի եղանակի պես ճգվում էր այդ շշունչը: Ջվարքը երևակայությամբ շոշում էր եղանակը, և սա ընդունում էր այն ընթացքը և այն բառերը, որ կամենում էր Ջվարքը:

Ջարթնեց Ջվարքը: Դեռ գիշեր էր: Անուշ քունը ետ էր քաշում նրան: Միայն մի անգամ աչքերը բացեց Ջվարքը և խցի դռան բացվածքից նայեց երկնքին: Լուսո աստղը հալած ոսկու պես դողում էր լուսացող, հում երկնակապույտի մեջ: Բայց այն հրաշալի շշունջը դեռ հոսում էր նրա ականջում:

Հետո կրկին զարթնեց: Ծիծեռը սաղմոսում էր վանքի քիվերում: Դա նույն այն շշունջն էր, որ քաղցր բարբառում էր:

Ջվարքը դուրս ելավ և գնաց անդնդի եզրը և սկսեց շրջել քարից քար: Արևի շողքերը դեռ նոր էին նկարում ժայռերի մռայլ սյուները: Դետև անդնդի միջով գնում էր իր օտար ճանապարհը: Նրա երգի մեջ լսվում էր երազի այն շշունջը:

Հանկարծ Ջվարքն անդրադարձավ «ո՞վ էր նա»... չէ՞ որ ինքը չէր: Բայց և ինչպես երազում մտածում էր, թե նա ինքն է: Ո՞վ էր նա...

Եվ նկատեց, որ ինքը շարունակում է այն շշունջը, որ ինքն է շշնջացողը։

Եվ իմացավ, որ երազի եակը ինքն է։ (Ախր երկու եակ չկա միևնույնը...)։

Եվ հանկարծ Չվարթը զարթնեց արթնության մեջ։ Նա զզաց խոսքը։ Նրա սիրտը մարեց մի անըմբռնելի տենչով։ Նա տենչաց խոսել, խոսել բարձր, երգաճայն, հանդիսավոր, թեկուզ բազմության առաջ։

Եվ սկսեց մի ասք մրմնջալ կիսաձայն։ Պատկերներ բազմաբրովանդակ։

Վանականները հավաքված էին գառան արևին, պարսպի տակ և դիտում էին ճորը։ Հանկարծ նրանք տեսան Չվարթին անդնդի վրա երերալիս.

— Գինով է, կգահավիժի անդունդը, — ճայնեց աբեղաներից մինը և վրա վազեց, բռնեց Չվարթին։

Չվարթը հրաբորբոք աչքերով նայեց նրանց և դողահար շրթունքները բաց սկսեց հնալ։ Նրան բերին վանահոր խուցի դուռը։ Վանահայրը դուրս եկավ.

— Ի՞նչ ունես, հիվա՞նդ ես, որդյա՛կ։

Բռնեց ճակատը։ Տաք էր։ Չվարթը հևում էր ինչպես տենդի մեջ և երազով նայում վանահորը։ Սա շոյեց նրա ճակատը և մեղմ հրամայեց.

— Խոսիր, որդյակ, ասա մեզ բան, ի՞նչ է մտածությու՞նը քո։

— Խոսի՛ր, խոսի՛ր, — պնդեցին աբեղաները։

Ջվարթը նայեց նրանց, վանահորը և հանկարծ փայլատակեց, սկսեց ոգել։ Ավելի հստակ զգաց, որ ինքը պիտի խոսի այն, որով լիքն է ինքը, սիրտ առավ և կրակվեց աշխուժով։ Նա սկսեց մի վեպ, թե ինչպես ինքը երազ տեսավ, ինչպես շնորհքն եկավ ու լցվեց իր մեջ, և որ ինքը կարող է ոգել, ինչ որ կամենա ամեն ոք։ Նա ոգում էր հափշտակված, բառերը անարգել հոսում էին, նա ոչինչ չէր տեսնում, — գալիս է գարունը, ձայն տալիս հողին, զարթնում է հողը, ձայն տալիս բոլոր բույսերին։ Զարթնում է ձնծաղիկը, ձայն տալիս մյուս ծաղիկներին, թե զարթեցեք, զարթեցեք, քանի քնեք հողում, զարթեցեք, լցրեք աշխարհը ուրախությամբ։

Սար ու ձոր լցվում է ծաղիկներով։
Եվ
Ծափ է տալիս ծափձափը, ծիծաղում,
Աշխարհը թագ է բոլորում գլխին,
Ղաթիֆան* հագնում է ծիրանի,
Ծառուրիկը** սուրմա քաշում աչքերին։
Եվ
Սեր է աշխարհին, սեր են մարդիկ,
Սեր է արևն, սեր՝ ծաղիկն,

---

* Ծաղիկ (այդ անվամբ եղել է նաև մետաքսյա կտոր, որից Կարնո կանայք կարել են իրենց տոնական զգեստները)։
** Ծաղկի տեսակ, տարածված Արևմտահայաստանում։

Սեր են հավքերն ամեն երկնուց,
Սիրով են ամենքը գեղեցիկ։

Վանականները լսում էին մթին քարերի պես, անարձագանք, սառն։ Միայն նրանցից ամենաչարը, տխմարադեմ Ազարիան, դառն ու նախանձահույզ ձայնով հարցրեց, բողոքեց։

— Որպես խոսի սա զբանս զայս, զի չէ սա վարդապետ։

Վանահայրը սաստեց նրան։

— Մի բանսարկիր։ Միտք նորա ինքնաբուխ են և պայծառ։ Եվ իմաստուն է պատանին այս, քան զվարդապետ։

Վանականները սաստված նայեցին Ջվարթին և պապանձվեցին։

Եվ նկատեց Ջվարթը — նախանձահույզ Ազարիան, որ դավ էր ուզում նյութել իր դեմ, նախանձից դեղնեց։ Սյուսները մռայլեցին, ոմանք ամաչեցին, իսկ ոմանք էլ շտապեցին խուսափել վանահոր աչքերից, թերևս նաև Ջվարթից։

Վանահայրը արձակեց Ջվարթին և վանականներին հրամայեց ցրվել իրենց խուցերը։ Նրանք հեռացան ռիսով ցված դեպի Ջվարթը։ Նրանք ատեցին Ջվարթին։ Եվ ամեն պատահելիս հարձակվում էին վրան, կշտամբում, բարկանում։ Ջվարթը չէր հասկանում նրանց, ժպտուն նայում էր և անցնում։

— Նա ծաղրի է մատնում մեզ, — փրփրալի ժայթքում են վանականները վանահոր վրա, որ նա իր պաշտպանության տակն է առել մի խելագարի:

Սկսեցին հալածանք բորբոքել նրա դեմ: Բանսարկեցին նրան «հերետիկոս է, չարի գործիք. դիվական գիրք է գրում նա, պետք է այրել այն»:

Վանահայրը լսեց այդ և շատ վշտացավ: Նա զզում էր իր մահը: — Ում պիտի մնան իր կիսավարտ մտքերն ու գործերը, իր կառուցումների ոգին: Դունկիանոսն անուսում է դեռ, Ջվարթը պատանի: Ում պիտի ավանդի իր կտակը: Չորս կողմը խավար, անապատ:

Մի օր վանականները Ազարիայի գլխավորությամբ պաշարեցին վանահոր խցի դուռը: Եկան պահանջելու, որ արտաքսի Ջվարթին, որովհետև նա պղծում է սրբավայրը դիվական մտքերով:

Վանահայրը դուրս եկավ խցից:

— Որն իրավամբ, ամբարիշտներ, — բողոքի և վշտի ձայնով հարցրեց նա, — տեսեք նրա շնորհքը, նրա մտքերը:

— Թող դուրս գա, խոսի կրկին, և մենք ցույց կտանք նրա մեղքը:

Վանահայրը դուրս կանչեց Ջվարթին:

— Ե՛կ, որդյակ, եկ արդարացիր:

Ջվարթը դուրս եկավ և ժպտալով նայեց վանականներին: Ահա դու առաջի մարդկան ասա մի բան, թող դատեն քեզ։ Զվարթը մտածեց մի փոքր և ապա կերպարանափոխվեց։ Նա սկսեց ոգել։ Ինչի՞ մասին էր այդ։

Բովանդակությունը այս էր։

Եկավ գարունը, ծաղիկները հորդեցին,
Մանիշակը ժողովեց բոլոր ծաղիկներին
Եվ դավ սարքեց վարդի հանդիման.
Վճռեցին սպանել վարդին, որ չլինի թե,
Գա զարդարվի վարդն կարմիր,
Ամենքի ուշը գրավի իր վրան,
Ամենքը նայեն վարդին կարմիր։
Եվ իրենք աննկատելի մնան։
Հորոտ-մորոտը ճայնեց ճնճաղիկին,
Ճնճաղիկը շուշանին,
Շուշանը նունուֆարին,
Սուսամբարին, նարգիզին
Եվ ինչ որ ծաղիկ կար երկրի երեսին,
Որ գնան կոտրեն վարդն կարմիր։
Հանկարծ հնչեց ճայնը բլբուլի,
Եվ վարդը զարթնեց մեջն իր կանաչ վրանի,
Հանեց իր կանաչ կապան,
Հագավ իր վառ ծիրանին։
Ծաղիկները փախան, ցրվեցին, ումանք ամոթից,

Ումանք շփոթված, ումանք սուգ մտան կապտեցին,
Ումանք երկյուղից դարձան դեղին:
Վարդը զարդարեց իր բուրաստանը, եկավ բլբուլը նստեց նրա մոտ, հարբեց նրա անուշ հոտից ու երգեց բարձրաձայն, թե

Սեր է ծառն, սեր ծաղիկն
Սեր է հավքի ճայնն ի ծառին,
Սեր է վարդն, սեր բլբուլն,
Սիրով է նստել վրա վարդին:
Եթե չլիներ սեր իմ սրտիս,
Չէի կախվի վարդի փշին,
Եթե սերն ինձնից գատվի,
Ի՞նչ կտանեն ցուրտն ու քամին:

Տենչում է վարդը բլբուլին, խնդրում է բլբուլին, որ համբուրի իրեն, և ցույց է տալիս սիրտը, մեջը դեղին: Դա իր վիշտն է: Եվ գանգատվում է.
Պիտի քաղեն տանեն իրեն
Եվ եփեն դեղ հիվանդներին,
Դրանից է սիրտը դեղին:

Ջվարքը վերջացրեց և նայեց վանականներին. նրանց աչքերի սպիտակուցները փայլուն դանակների նման մերկացել էին իր դեմ:

Առաջ եկավ նախանձափրփուր Ազարիան, բացեց իր դառն բերանը և սկսեց բանսարկել.

— Մարմնավորաց են բանք վարդիս և սեր աշխարհի է:

— Պիղծ են բանք դորա,— մռմռացին մյուս վանականները:

— Մի բանսարկեք, մաքուր են մտածությունք պատանվույն:

Սակայն Ազարիան չսանձահարվեց: Նա ապերասան և կոկոզավիզ առաջ եկավ:

— Դիվահար է, հարկ է սպանանել զնա և դեն, որ է ի նմա,— գոռաց նա դառնաշունչ և կատաղի եզան նման հարու տվեց Ջվարթի վրա:

— Հեռու, խավարի ծնունդ,— բարձրացրեց ձեռքը վանահայրը,— որո՞ իրավամբ սպանես զանմեղն:

Բայց անհանգստացավ վանահայրը: Խռովություն էր բռնկվում: Պետք էր փրկել պատանուն կատաղած մոլեռանդներից: Ի՞նչ աներ... Նա հավատով նայեց Ջվարթին:

— Կարո՞ղ ես խոսել բան մեկնության,— խնդրող հրամայեց վանահայրը:

Ջվարքը թափանցեց նրա հոգու տագնապի մեջ, մի վայրկյան թափառեց մտքերի աշխարհը և ետ եկավ լարված ու վստահ:

Ու սկսեց:

Ասեմ ով է վարդն կարմիր,
Կամ ով են ծաղկունքն ամեն,
Կամ թե ով է բլբուլը քաջ,
Կամ թե որն է ճայն բլբուլի։

Ծաղկունք քահանայքն են հին օրինի, վարդը՝ Հիսուսը, մանիշակը՝ Հուդան, որ դավեց նրան և բլբուլը Գաբրիելն էր, որ փողը փչեց։ Վարդը, որ հագավ ծիրանին, Քրիստոսն էր, որ հարություն առավ, ծաղկունքը, որ թառամեցին, դեղնեցին, զինվորներն էին, որ փախան նրա գերեզմանից։

Գոհունակ ունկնդրեց վանահայրը, վանականները պապանձվեցին։ Զվարթը հաղթել էր։

Սակայն Ազարիան Զվարթի աչքերում նկատեց չարաճճի մի շող, ճարտար մտքի ճարպիկ խաղ։ Նա զգում էր, որ Զվարթի միտքը «մարմնավորաց» էր։ Բայց իր բութ միտքը չեր ծաղկում այնպես ճարտար, որ կարողանար հակաճառել։ Խավրեց նա քարայրի պես և ետ քաշվեց։ Գնացին և մյուսները։

Այնուհետև ամբողջ օրը խցերից լսվում էին անեծքի դառնաշունչ ճայներ։ Վանահայրն անձկության մեջ էր։ Զգում էր այս ամենի վախճանը։

Մի գիշեր՝ երկար գրում էր նա իր գրքի շարունակության մեջ։ Գրում էր իր կտակը։ Նա դառնացած էր վանականների բանսարկու և նախանձահույզ հալածանքից։

Նա իր կտակի մեջ ճաղկում էր մարդկային տգիտությունը, գովերգում էր ճշմարտությունը:

«...Անեանա մարմինն իմ որպես ծուխ և մնան միտք իմ ճշմարտության: Դուք կողդանաք իմ մարմինը, գրիվ կտաք որպես խռիվ, բայց իմ միտքը կմնա որպես լույսն արեգական: Մի դիպչեք ինձ, որդիք խավարի, — սպառնում էր նա իր կտակի մեջ, — ճշմարտությունն եմ ես և ես վրեժխնդիր կլինեմ ճեզանից»:

Գրեց մինչև խորին գիշեր: Լուսաբացին զարթեցրեց Ջվարթին և Դունկիանոսին, մոտ կանչեց, համբուրեց նրանց և ասաց, որ գնում է:

— Ո՞ւր, — հարցրեց Դունկիանոսը, բայց և իսկույն հասկացավ և դառնորեն լացեց:

Վանահայրն իր նվիրական գիրքը հանձնեց պատանիներին և պատվիրեց լավ պահպանել: Եվ մեռավ:

Վանահորը թաղեցին բռնաղատված շուքով, բայց խորին ատելությամբ:

Դունկիանոսը նրա գիրքը գաղտնի տարավ Թադեի մոտ, և նրանք թաղեցին քարե գաղտնարանում:

Հետևյալ օրը վանականները Ջվարթին փակեցին մի մութ խցիկում և թույլ չտվին երգելու ծաղիկների երգը: Նրան այցելում էր միայն Դունկիանոսը: Ջվարթը թախիծով նայում էր նրան և սկսում խոսել, ոգել իր վեպը: Դունկիանոսը լսում էր, լսում և երկուսով մոռանում, որ

30

բանտի մեջ էին։ Սիրում էր Ղունկիանոսը լսել այդ վեպը։

Բայց մի օր էլ նրան արգելեցին այցելել Զվարթին։ Այնուհետև Ղունկիանոսը գալիս էր բանտի լուսամուտից նայելու, գլուխը ծռած, տրտում։ Ժպտում էր Զվարթը և նայում երազով, կարծես անհոգ։

Եվ մեռավ Զվարթն այդպես, հոգում ծաղիկներ։

Ավերակ վանքի խարխուլ խցում արշող կյանք է ծաղկում։ Այնտեղ Թադեն հողի հատակին արևի պես սփռում է գույներ, լույսեր, խաղեր։ Առաստաղից, կաշվե բարակ թելերից տախտակներ են կախ, վրաները մագաղաթ քաշած։ Թաթախում է Թադեն սուր գրիչը երանգապանակի մեջ և արծվի աչքերը մագաղաթին անշարժանում է, սպասում և հանկարծ այծամորուքը կախելով մագաղաթի էջին սրբությամբ ծաղկում է էջը։ Պատանիներ այծյամի աչքերով նայում են իրենց վարպետին։ Վախենում են նրանից և սիրում նրան։ Թադեն հրաշքներ է գործում իր գրչով։ Քանի մռայլում է նա, այնքան ժպտում են մագաղաթները։ Այնտեղ է Ղունկիանոսը։ Նրա աչքերը գնում են կորչում այդ ծաղկած մագաղաթների ոսկու, լաջվարդի, նարնջի, հակինթի մեջ։

Հարցնում է, — ի՞նչ գիրք է այս։

Թադեն վեր նայեց։ Նրա աչքերը խորն են հորիզոնի պես։ Նա նոր տեսավ Ղունկիանոսին և արթնացավ։ Երազի մեջ էր։

Նա կրկին կոացավ մագաղաթի վրա։ Նրա աչքը մի սիրամարգի կողմն էր, որի սրճագույն գլուխն ու վիզը հոխորտ կարկառել էր վերև և գետնի վրա սփռել էր փետուրների ասեղնագործ գորգը։ Մանվածապատ հակինթների ու գոհարների ցոլքով խաղում են լուսանցքին։ Իսկ վերևը՝ աստեղալույց երկնքում այնպիսի մի երկնակապույտ է, որ կարծես մագաղաթը ճեղքել էր և ինքը երկինքն էր նայում այնտեղից։

Աշակերտները լուրկ ու հնազանդ լցնում էին ծաղկող վարպետի շրջանակները հավելյալ մանրամասներով։

Երբեմն Թադեն հայացքը շրջեցնում էր դեպի աշակերտները և իր նաղաշական հրահանգներն էր տալիս նրանց։

— Ոսկեձույլ նշողն ընդ նարնջին... ծաղիկ ընդ ծաղկանց... բոլորակն ոսկեճաճանչ, կամարն երկնահան գույն... Պայծառ լաջվարդույք, նոճին կանաչագեղ, թագագլուխ վարդն — այս է կանոնն...

Գիշեր է։ Թադեի խցում Ղունկիանոսը պատմում է Զվարթի կյանքը։ Թադեն լսում է։ Մոլի է նա, արբած՝ իր գույներով, բայց գիշերվա մթնում չի կարող ծաղկել։ Քունը չի տանում, քունը փախցրել են երանգները, որ վառվում են խավարի սև պաստառի վրա։ Բնությունն է միայն, որ նկարում է երկնքի էջի վրա, սփռում ծաղիկների թերթեր։ Թադեն լսում է։

Ղունկիանոսը ոգեց Զվարթի երգը ծաղիկների մա-

սին։ ╳Խեղճ Ղունկիանոս, միայն մի հստակ հիշողություն ունի այս աշխարհում և բարի սիրտ)։

Նա ոգեց գեղջուկ ճայնով և անկեղծ շեշտով։ Թադեն ականջները սրեց։ Լսեց, լսեց և գլուխն օրորեց։

— Երանի, երանի, երանի, անո՜ւշ է սրտին։

— Ծաղկիր ✡Զվարթի վեպը, վարպետ, — ասաց Ղունկիանոսը արտասվելով։

Վարպետը ցնցվեց։

— Ճշմարիտն ասացիր, վաղիվն իսկ կսկսեմ։ Երանի թե կարենամ։

րքրտված տանջվում է Նադաշը։ Ծաղկում է Ջվարթի վեպը վանահոր գրքի մեջ։ Նայում է Ղունկիանոսը Նադաշին խոնարհ ու ջերմեռանդ։ Սա խառնում է գույնը գույնին, խառնում, թողնում ու կրկին, կրկին։ Կրակներ են վառվում մագաղաթի ճակատին ու լուսանցքներին։ Բոցագույն վագրեր թռել են նարնջենի եղնիկների մեջքին և պատրաստվում են հոշոտելու նրանց։ Դողահար է նկարում Նադաշը, նա թվում է մոլի, խելագար։ Ինչ որ հիվանդագին ջերմի մեջ, նա հատնում է մոմի պես, որոնում է մի շատ դժվար նրբերանգ։ Գույնը չի գտնվում։ Նրա աչքերը մարեցին, կիսախուփ նայել սկսեցին կարծես մի անդունդ, որի հատակին վառվում է մի հազվագյուտ ծաղիկ, աներևակայելի նրբերանգով։ Ու հենց այն է, գրիչը թաթախեց պնակի մեջ և դրեց մագաղաթի վրա, նրբերանգը փախավ ինչպես շնաշխարհիկ թռչուն։ Նաղաշը հոգոց հանեց և հուսահատ նայեց դռնից դուրս։ Աշակերտները պապանձվեցին, նայեցին իրենց վարպետին և ակնածանքով սպասեցին։ Նրանք ապրեցին վարպետի տանջանքը։

Հանկարծ Նաղաշը սրտնեղած վեր կացավ և լուռ, լուսնոտի պես գնաց դուրս, անցավ գավիթը և հեռացավ։

— Գնաց երանգը գտնելու, գնանք հետևից։

Աշակերտները և Ղունկիանոսն էլ նրանց հետ դուրս եկան։ Նաղաշը գնում էր դաշտը։ Ամբողջ օրը թափառեց նա իր աշակերտների հետ։ Մոտեցավ, նայեց նկարին։ Հետո վերցրեց գրիչը։ Պատանիները քարացան։ Սրբագան լռության մեջ ժպտաց մագաղաթը։

Ոսկեհուր մի գիրք, լի լույսերով և իմաստությամբ։ Բոցավառ կենդանաբյուններ, ճկնազազաններ և ծաղիկներ շրջանակել են երկու վեպ. մեկը՝ որ խոսում է աշխարհի կառուցողական սկզբունքի, շինարարական աշխատանքի սրբության մասին, իսկ մյուսը, որ կրակե ժապավենի նման հոսում է էջե էջ— Ձվարթի վեպը ծաղիկների մասին։

յուն է թափվում լույսի նման: Բայց սև է վանքը և մութ նկուղը, որի մեջ բանտարկված է ձեռագիրների հետ մի գիրք և ոչնչանում է խոնավից: Ասում են այդպես է լինում միշտ — ոչնչանում են մագաղաթները խոնավից: Այդ գրքում ծաղիկներ կան: Արդյոք քնե՞լ են ծաղիկները գրքի մեջ, թե ոչնչանում են նաև նրանք:

Վանականները պորտաբույծ կյանք են վարում: Նրանք փքվել են գործերի պես ու մոռացել Զվարթին, վանահորը, Թադեին և նրա աշակերտներին: Նրանց բոլորին քշել են վանքից, նրանք ցրված են ով գիտե ուր:

իշեր: Ձմեռը մրրկում է: Մրրկում է Հայաստանի լեռնաշխարհում: Ցուրտ է, երկինքը սառ ապակի: Լեռների լանջերով գնում է Ղունկիանոսը, մեջքին մի պարկ, ձեռին մի մռոտ մետաքսե կապոց: Նրա կարկամած ձեռները կապտել են, բայց նա մատները երկաթի պես գամել է գրքի կազմին, որ մետաքսի տակից սառը կծում է: Կսառեն այդ մատները, և նա գիրքը ձեռքից բաց չի թողնի: Նա փախել է մենաստանից: Միայն մի բան գիտե, որ գրքերն է ազատում: Միայն թե ազատվեն նրանք... Ո՞ւր է գնում, ինքն էլ չգիտե: Աշխարհավեր մրրիկ է լեռնաշխարհում: Զորքեր են հոսում հովիտներում: Այրվում են քաղաքներ, գյուղեր, վանքեր, գրադարաններ:

Առավոտյան դեմ բուքը բերանքսիվայր ընկավ դաշտերի ու լեռների վրա: Մի խարխուլ լեռնավանքի դռան, որ մի ծեր վանական բաց էր արել, ձյան մեջ մի կիսաթաղ մարդ է երևում, պարկը մեջքին, կողքին մետաքսախառն մի գիրք, որ բացվել է և ժպտում կապույտ երկնքին:

Ծեր վանականը նայեց գրքին և վերցրեց դողահար:

ավար մի ամպ շղարշում է գիրքը և նրա պատմությունը: Մի դարու պատմություն:
Ոչինչ չի երևում ուրիշ: Մի փոքրիկ բացվածք միայն թույլ է տալիս նշմարելու մի բեկոր:
Զրնգում են ճանապարհները սուլթան էլտըրըմի հետևազնդերի սմբակներից:
Կարկուտ-ամպի պես է գնում նա սրընթաց: Պապանձվել է երկիրը, էլտըրըմն է լսվում միայն:
Վանքի մի խցում նստել է մի ծերուկ, գրքեր է քննում խորասույզ: Խուլ է նա դեպի արհավիրքը: Կարդում է: Ներս են գալիս երկու զինվոր: Չի նկատում նրանց: Չայն են տալիս նրանք: Չի լսում: Չայրանում են զինվորները և նետահարում ծերունուն: Նա ընկնում է:
Մի փոքր անց, կրակն սկսեց լափել գրքերը: Ճանճա-

հում ծանր, դառն: Մագաղաթները կշրտում են: Զինվորները տաքանում են, զվարճանում գրքերի ճարճատյունից: Հետո հանգստացան, կշտացան, նայեցին չորս կողմ, ծերունուն: Նայեցին անշար աչքերով, երկյուղած: Զգում են, զուր սպանեցին նրան:
— Ի՞նչ գրքեր են սրանք:
— Ո՞վ գիտե...
— Ասում են գիրքը զայրանում է, պատժում... Նրանց մեջ ճշմարտությունն է գրած: (Խեղճ զինվոր, միայն գրքի մեջ, թե նաև իր մեջ...):
Հանկարծ մի գիրք պայթեց ու թռավ մի կողմ կրակից: Դիպված շեր — մագաղաթ, յուղ, կրակ... Բայց ցնցվեցին և վրա ընկնելով կրակին հանգցրին: Գրքերը միայլ սկսեցին ծանր, դառն:
Դուրս ընկան ճանապարհի:
— Գիրքը զայրացավ:
— Այո, գիրքը չի կարելի վառել:

որում սոսափեցին ութինները, մտածեցին և կրկին սոսափեցին։ Հետո պաղ գետի պես ճորավերևից հոսեց աշունը և գնաց ճորնիվայր։ Սոսափին խառնվեց և մի ուրիշ սոսափ։ Դա ջրաղացի բանդի մամռահոտ ջուրն էր։ Բաց թողեց ջրաղացպան Հակոբը բանդի ջուրը։ — Էլ կարիք չկա նավերից ջուրը հոսեցնելու։

Սով է համայն երկրում։

Հակոբը ուշենու տակ խորհուրդ արեց իր երիտասարդ որդու հետ։

— Գնա, Հուսիկ, Դամասկոս։ Աղորիքները կանգնեցին։ Գնա ցորեն բեր, ցանենք, կենդանությունը շմարի։

Հուսիկի կապույտ աչքերը թախծալի ժպտացին։ Նա կրկնեց։

— Կենդանություն:

Ու բերանաբաց ժպիտով նայեց հորը:

— Ի՞նչ ես հիմար մտիկ տալիս: Խելքդ գլուխդ հավաքիր, երկիրը կործանվում է:

Հակոբը մտավ ջրաղաց, հանեց անկյունից մի ծաղկավոր խալաթ, հինգ մետաքս թաշկինակ և հետո կաշվե մատներով շոշափեց ու քսակից հանեց երեսուն դահեկան:

— Տասը բահ եմ շինել — նրա գինն է: Խալաթը ծախելով ճանապարհը կկտրես, մի քիչ էլ կբանես, կբերես, գառնան մի բան գցենք հողին բերանը: Կենդանությունը չմարի:

Հուսիկը նայում է հոր աչքերին: Հայրը ազդում է նրան բնության նման: Նա ինչ-որ խորը, սարսափելի բան է ասում:

Հուսիկը ճանապարհ ընկավ դեպի Դամասկոս:

Գնում է Հուսիկը մի կապույտ, տրտմալի ժպիտ աչքերում: Հեռավոր կապույտը, հեռավոր հայրենիքի:

Հրաշեկ ճանապարհներ են կտրում երկիրը: Նրանք տանում են բուրայի հակեր՝ արմավի, գորենի, փստոցի, սուրճի:

Գնում է Հուսիկը, կարծես աշխարհի վրայով և մտածում է: Եվ յուրովի ժպտում է չարածճիորեն.

— Ի՞նչ էր ասում հայրը՝ «Կենդանությունը չմարի»: Ո՞վ, ի՞նչը կկրկի մարդուն: Հողը, կիսեն: Ամիրան իր գործերով, նրա դեմ կանգնած են սեղջուկների, թաթարների իշխանները, հեղեղ հեղեղի միջով գալիս են լափում, ջնջում իրար։ Գուցե հարստությունն, բայց տեսավ Հուսիկը, թե ինչպես մերկացան հարուստները, ոսկին գնաց, մնացին կմախքները։ Ուրեմն ի՞նչը կապահի կենդանությունը, ո՞րն է վեմը կենդանության։

Վեմը, — ահա թե ի՞նչ է որոնում Հուսիկի միտքը։

Ու երերում է Հուսիկը քրտնախաշ, ազազիլ տատասկի պես արևի դեղին ծովի մեջ։

— Ա՜յ, եթե մարդ թռչուն դառնար, փախցներ իր հետ ոսկին, հացը, զգեստը, կյանքը։ — Բայց ի՞նչ օգուտ, անգղներն ու արծիվները երկնքում կբզկտեին մարդուն և կհափշտակեին նրա բոլոր ինչքը։

Ոսկեփոշի քաղաքը հուրիրատում էր արևի լույսով։ Մի հախուռն բազմություն եռում է այնտեղ։ Հուսիկի աչքերը խայտացին, շլացան։ Ահա մի կրակոտ երիտասարդ բրոնզե ձեռքերն օդի մեջ, ծռում է մի հրացայտ սուր։ Պողպատը ցնցվում է ու շիտակվում օձի պես։ Նրան շրջապատել են պղնձե երիտասարդները։ Նրանք ծիծաղում են սաղաշի ատամներով։ Ուղտեր են ջոքել շինարների շուրջը, նրանց կողքին ցաքուցրիվ հակերն են գորենի ու բյուր բարիքների։

Նստեց հոգնած այդ հակերի մոտ, մեջքը տվեց չինարու բնին։ Արևը կիզում է նրան, տոթը խեղդում։ Նայում է շուկան շրջանակած տներին, մարդկանց —

43

բոլորը խանձված են բարկ արևից։ Կապուտակ ջրերի կոհակներ վետվետացին Հուսիկի աչքերում։ Նա անգամ զգաց նրանց սառցի շրթերը իր պապակ շուրթերին։ Քուն է գալիս աչքերին։ Նայում է մշուշոտ հայացքով։ Երկար էր նայում, քնել էր և զարթնել, չէր հիշում․ նայեց և ահա տեսավ իր դեմ մի խառնված բազմություն, որ ծիծաղելով իրար ձեռքից առնում և բարկ մատներով կոպիտ բացուխուփի էին անում մի գիրք։ Հուսիկը վեր կացավ, գրավվելով ինչ-որ ծանոթ բանով։ Ի՞նչ է դա։ Այո, այդ գրքի տեսքը։ Նա տեսել է դրանցից։ Մոտեցավ։ Անզգույշ, կոշտ եղունգներ քերում էին գրքի կողերը։ Մի ուրիշ ձեռք խլեց գիրքը և ինքը սկսեց տնտղել նրա սևակազմ, արծաթ պատյանը։ Հետո բացեց գիրքը և նայեց էջերին։

Գարուններ բացվեցին և մրգահաս աշուններ, երկինքներ սուտակ, բուրաստաններ, հրեղեն վարդեր, վագրեր ոսկեձույլ և ծաղիկներ մանվածապատ, ջերմ, հափշտակված, հրճվալից։ Հուսիկի աչքերում նկարվեցին իր լեռների, հովիտների մոթիմ գույները։

Ի՞նչ էր գրած այս գրքում, որ այդպես չերմագին ծաղկազարդված էր։ Գիրքը ծախում էին։ Ծախողը մի արաբ զինվոր էր, բարեդեմ ու անհոգ։ Նա ձեռք էր բերել այդ իրը արշավանքի ժամանակ և հիմարություն էր արել բերելու մինչև Դամասկոս... «Ինչի՞ն էր պետք»։

— Հը՛, ի՞նչ տամ, — բերանը ծիծաղով ծռում է մի ուրախ մարդ։

— Երեսուն դահեկան*։

Գնորդը փռթկաց, և գիրքը թռավ, ընկավ գետին, փոշու մեջ։ Սյուսներր ռտներով խփեցին այս ու այն կողմ։ Ջինվորը ծիծաղեց, գնաց ծույլորեն վերցրեց գիրքը և բռնեց ձեռին։ Զվարճանում է, որ ինքը ծախում է, նրանք էլ չեն առնում։

Հուսիկը մոտ գնաց և գիրքը շոշափեց։ Տաք էր արծաթը նրա մատների մեջ։ Բացեց գիրքը։ Նայեց նրան թեթև, հանդարտ։ Աչքեր երևացին ծաղիկների միջից։ Մի գառնանային իմաստություն, մի հարատև կենդանություն բուրեց նրանց միջից։ Գիրքը հանգիստ էր մի մարդու նման, որ գիտե կյանքի բոլոր օրենքները և կենդանության գաղտնիքը և չի վախենում մահից, սիրում է կյանքը և հավատով է ճակատագրի դեմ։ Հուսիկը հեգելով կարդաց․ «Չի աշխատք սուրբ են»։

Հուսիկը հիշեց, հիմա միայն հիշեց, իր գինեսեր ու զվարթ Սարգիս ապուպապին, որի մասին ասել էին, որ մի առույգ որմնադիր էր եղել։ Երգում էր եղել «բանելիս», երգում՝ աղետների օրերին և երբեք չէր ծերանում։ Մի անգամ գործից վերադառնալով նա տեսել էր, որ իր տունը կողոպտել էին։ Ճիպ մերկացավ ընտանիքը։ Բայց Սարգիս ապուպապը քահ-քահ ծիծաղել էր․

— Ձեռքս չեն գողացել։

---

* Դրամական միավոր մահմեդական աշխարհում։

Ամենանեղ օրերին նա միշտ ասելիս էր եղել. «Կաշխատենք-կապրենք»:

Այս էր ասել նաև նրա որդին երևելի կառուցող, սրա որդին և վերջինի որդին Հուսիկի հայրը: Եվ ասել էր հայրը, լսել էր սրա հայրը, և սա էլ լսել էր իր հորից, որ ամենամեծ բանն աշխարհում աշխատանքն է:

«Աշխատանքը սուրբ է» — այսպես է գրած գրքում, ասելիս են եղել Հուսիկի պապերը — բոլորն աշխատավոր: Կրկին կարդաց.

— «Ջի աշխատք սուրբ են»:

Ուրեմն սա այն գիրքն է...

Հուսիկի աչքերը վառվում են և միտքը կորչում հեռուն...

Նա հանեց իր դրամները և տվեց զինվորին: Սա վերցրեց, գիրքը աշխույժ խոթեց Հուսիկի բուռը և ծիծաղելով գնաց: Ծիծաղեցին նրա հետևից մյուսներն և զարմացած նայեցին Հուսիկին:

Սա երազում էր:

Մոտեցան ուրիշ օտար մարդիկ, նայեցին գրքին, Հուսիկին: Ու մինչ սա գիրքը դնում էր իր տոպրակը, մի ծանոթ ձայն սթափեցրեց նրան, Սողոմոնն էր, իր հայրենակիցը:

— Դու խելառ ես, թե՞ հիմար: Փողդ տվիր գրքին:

— Հա, — կտրած ժպիտով, փոքր-ինչ հիմար նայում է Հուսիկը Սողոմոնին:

— Ապա գառնան ի՞նչ ես ցանելու։

Հուսիկը ապուշ նայում է և աչքերում առկայծում է թախծալի մի շող։

Շփոթված է, թե կատակ էր արեց։

— Հիմա գնա տուն, անխելք։

Կգնա տուն և սովը նստած կլինի այնտեղ։ Մոխրագույն մի անդունդ է ընկղմում գիրքը։ էլ ոչինչ չի երևում։

Ի՞նչ եղավ Հուսիկը, ինչպես վերապրեց սովը։ Ալ-սինքն մահը։ Խեղճ, խեղճ Հուսիկ...

Գրքի հիշատակարանում գրած է, թե ինչպես նա դրամը տվեց գրքի դիմաց... երևի կարծելով, որ գրեհն անգամ կենդանություն չէ, որ անգամ նա չի փրկի իր կյանքը մահից։

իվանդ երեխայի բարձի տակից (ահռելիորեն ծանր շարժվել, բայց անցել են կրկին դարեր), կյանքի հուսով նայում է նա, այն գիրքը։ Ի՞նչ գիրք է, ոչ ոք չգիտե անգրագետ հողագործի այս ընտանիքում։ Նրան գտել են մի ավերակ տան մոխրանոցում։ Ասում են բժշկում է ամեն հիվանդություն։ Երեխան հոգու հիվանդություն ունի...

 — Ի՞նչ քարավան է, ո՞ւր էսպես, Խոջա՛։
— Վենետիկ, Ճենովա, թե բարին աջողդի։

Խոջան կբել է, կարդում է անվերջ, շիկափուկ ճանապարհի եզրին։ Ուղտերի բեռներում՝ որդանկարմիր, տորոն, մորթիներ, ակնեղեն։

Քարավանը հանգչում է։ Ուղտերը որոճում են։
Կարդում է Խոջան և վանում ճանապարհի թախիծը։

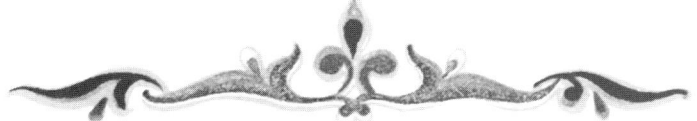

Լ դարերի խորքից գալիս է մի գիրք: Խավարի միջին թափառող լույսի է նման դողդողում է, բայց գալիս է. թե ինչ վտանգներ է անցնում, չի տեսնում նա: Ո՛չ ձմեռ, ո՛չ խավար: Ոչ կրակն է այրում նրան, ոչ շոգը խեղդում: Հրաշքն է պահում նրան, թե պատահմունքը: Բայց սերունդները խնամում են նրան, թաքցնում, փրկում և ավանդում նրան հետնորդներին, ձեռքե-ձեռք անցկացնում դարերի փորձանքներից, անցկացնում հուր, սուր, ջուր:

Ժպտում է գիրքը: Սիամիտ է նա, անհոգ է նա, խորամանկ է նա և գիտե՛ իր գործը կարգադրել: Թե իմաստուն է, հայտնի է իրեն իր ճանապարհի գիրքը:

Նման արևի լույսին, որ անհոգ խաղում է փրփրած ծովի կատաղի ալիքների վրա։ Դեղնում են ալիքները, կապտում, փրփրալի ժայթքում, գոչում, բռնցքում արևի դեմ, բայց նա ժպտում է։ Վտանգ չի իմանում նա, ատելություն չի դիպչում նրան, ալիք չի փշրում նրան։

Հազար ձեռքեր պահել, շոյել, շոշափել են այս ծաղիկները՝ կյանքի գեղեցկությունը, հազար-հազար աչքեր նայել են նրանց հետևից սիրով ու թախիծով։ Մոխրացել են հազար ձեռքեր, տենչալի աչքեր, և մնացել է այս ջերմ գիրքը։

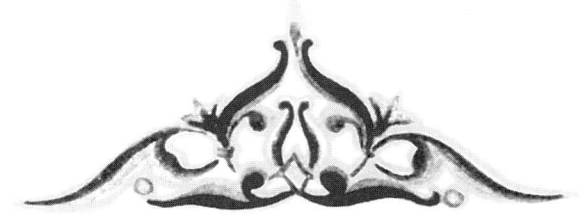

Նաշնչվում է մի ամբողջ ժողովուրդ։ Ոչ թե մի գիրք։ Թնդանոթներն ահեղ վիճակում են, «նա կորած է»... — ոչ, «նա փրկված է», «...հրաշք է, թե փրկվի...»։

Կարմիր հողմ փոթորկալի թերթում է ոսկելույս թերթերը գրքի, որ ընկած մի մեծ ճանապարհի վրա նայում է նրան մտերմորեն։ Նա փրկված է իրեն միշտ փրկող ժողովրդի հետ։ Երկաթե գրադարաններում լռում են դարերը։ Մի ալեհեր գլուխ հակված է պատմության անդունդը և խոր հովտում տեսնում է ծաղիկներ, ծաղիկներ, ծաղիկներ...

ԴԵՐԵՆԻԿ ԴԵՄԻՐՃՅԱՆ
Գիրք ծաղկանց
(պատմվածք)

ДЕРЕНИК ДЕМИРЧЯН
Книга цахканц
(рассказ)
(На армянском языке)
Издательство «Советакан грох»
Ереван, 1985

Խմբագիր՝ Ռ. Մ. Մուրադյան
Գեղ. խմբագիր՝ Գ. Խ. Գյուլամիրյան
Տեխ. խմբագիր՝ Ս. Մ. Սիմոնյան
Վերստուղող սրբագրիչ՝ Հ. Ն. Զորյան

ИБ 4552

Հանձնված է շարվածքի 04.08.84։ Ստորագրված է տպագրության 20.04.85։ Ֆորմատ 70X108I/₃₂։ Թուղթ օֆսեթ։ Տառատեսակ՝ «Արարատ»։ Տպագրություն օֆսեթ, 2,45 պյմ. տպ. մամ., 10,13 պյմ. ներկ. թերթ., 1,68 հրատ. մամ.։ Տպաքանակ 50 000։ Պատվեր 3251։ Գինը 20 կոպ., ցելոֆանով 25 կոպ. (10 000 օրինակ)

«Սովետական գրող» հրատարակչություն, Երևան — 9, Տերյան 91։
Издательство «Советакан грох», Ереван-9, ул. Теряна, 91.

ՀՍՍՀ հրատարակչությունների, պոլիգրաֆիայի և գրքի առևտրի գործերի պետական կոմիտեի գունավոր տպագրության տպարան, Երևան — 82, Ադմիրալ Իսակովի պող. 48։
Типография цветной печати Госкомитета по делам издательств, полиграфии и книжной торговли Арм. ССР, Ереван —82, пр. Адмирала Исакова, 48.